THE REALLY USEFUL
ULTIMATE
STUDENT
COOK
BOOK

SILVANA FRANCO

MURDOCH BOOKS

Published by Murdoch Books Pty Limited

Murdoch Books Australia
Pier 8/9, 23 Hickson Road, Millers Point NSW 2000
Phone: +61 (0) 2 8220 2000   Fax: +61 (0) 2 8220 2558

Murdoch Books UK Limited
Erico House, 6th Floor, 93-99 Upper Richmond Road
Putney, London SW15 2TG
Phone: +44 (0) 20 8785 5995   Fax: + 44 (0) 20 8785 5985

Chief Executive: Juliet Rogers
Publisher: Kay Scarlett
Concept: James Mills-Hicks
Design: Peta Nugent, Jenny Cowan
Production: Kita George

Printed in Hong Kong by Sing Cheong Printing Company Limited.
Reprinted 2007, 2008.

ISBN 978 1 74196 024 2

RECIPE NOTES

(REALLY EASY) Degree of difficulty

(35 MINUTES) Approximate time required to prepare and cook each recipe.

(SERVES 2) Indicates serving size

(V) Indicates dishes that are suitable for vegetarians

IMPORTANT: Those who might be at risk from the effects of salmonella poisoning
(the elderly, pregnant women, young children and those suffering from immune deficiency
diseases) should consult their doctor with any concerns about eating raw eggs.

CONVERSION GUIDE: You may find cooking times vary depending on the oven you are
using. For fan-forced ovens, as a general rule, set the oven temperature to 20°C (70°F)
lower than indicated in the recipe. We have used 20 ml (4 teaspoon) tablespoon measures.
If you are using a 15 ml (3 teaspoon) tablespoon, for most recipes the difference will not
be noticeable. However, for recipes using baking powder, gelatine, bicarbonate of soda,
small amounts of flour and cornflour (cornstarch), add an extra teaspoon for each
tablespoon specified.

CONTENTS

INTRODUCTION

Becoming a student usually means leaving home, and for the first time being completely responsible for your own money, cleaning, washing and of course, cooking. Bearing in mind that time and money are of the essence, you may think that bothering to cook for yourself is a waste of precious time and energy that could be better spent surfing the net, studying or drinking. But there are a few very good reasons why you should take the time to cook and eat properly.

You need a balanced, healthy diet to function to the best of your ability both physically and mentally. Cooking your own food from scratch is cheaper and healthier than ready-made meals and take-away food. If you have the added complication of being a non-meat eater then eating well can be a minefield. It is very easy for the young veggie to live on cheese and eggs which although may ensure an adequate intake of protein will lead to weight gain, high cholesterol levels, and the lack of other essential vitamins and minerals. Not only is cooking your own food from scratch the cheapest and healthiest option, it also means you can be sure of exactly what you are eating. It's also great fun. Invite friends for a meal and impress them with your inventiveness and creativity, and don't forget, if you're living in a shared house full of students, as the cook, you get to skip the washing up.

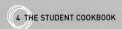

This is a basic book, with dishes that you will be able to master even if you've never boiled an egg before. All the recipes are very straightforward, giving plenty of scope for you to adapt them and make them your own. Save time in the kitchen by being well prepared and planning what you're going to cook in advance. If your cupboard is well stocked, you should be able to knock up a meal for two without having to go out for extra ingredients as most of the recipes in this book serve two. If you're only cooking for yourself, it's still worth making the full quantity and then reheating it the next day or taking it to college with you for your lunch.

A good time-saving way to balance your meals is to cook all-in-one complete meals based on a carbohydrate such as pasta or rice. To help you stick to these guidelines this book includes chapters based upon the four main carbohydrates. If you make dishes that need an accompaniment, steam some fresh vegetables or make a quick salad rather than choosing chips. See page 6 for nutritional information which includes more details on meal planning. Happy cooking!!

EATING WELL

Eating well is the key to getting the best from life. If you plan to cram your revision or study late into the night, it is essential that you eat a well-balanced diet that will not only keep your mind and body fuelled, but can also help prevent heart disease, tooth decay and obesity as well as many other common illnesses. Studies have shown, for example, that you're less likely to get a cold if you have a good intake of vitamin C, which is something to think about if you've got exams looming.

Generally speaking, the more varied your diet, the more likely it is that all the vital nutrients you need are being provided. In order to ensure you are getting enough, you must be eating from each of the three main food groups detailed below. Having discovered how to plan good balanced meals you should also take a look at the snacks you eat between meals. Try to drink plenty of water and eat yogurts or fruit if you get hunger pangs – sugary drinks and fried salty snacks will just help you to pile on the pounds, and offer very little by way of nutrients.

GROUP 1

CARBOHYDRATES

Starchy foods like potatoes and bread are good sources of fibre, vitamins and minerals. Carbohydrates like these should be the base of every meal. They are naturally low in fat (and as a nation, we consume far more fat than we need), and will satisfy your hunger.

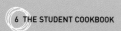

Your body needs carbohydrates to convert into energy but there are two main types: starch and sugar. When you eat a sugar-filled food or drink, you get an almost instant energy surge, which is quickly followed by a low. Your brain tells you that you need more energy and you crave for another bar of chocolate or can of fizzy pop. Yo-yoing energy levels can leave you feeling lethargic and unable to concentrate on your studies. Because starches are digested by the body far more slowly than sugars, they give a constant slow-releasing source of energy which is exactly what you need if you're going into a three-hour exam. If you have a heavy day ahead, you must eat a proper breakfast. When you wake up, your sugar levels are low so boost them up with sustaining food. Have a couple of slices of toast and Marmite or Vegemite and a big bowl of muesli or porridge, avoid tea or coffee and have a glass of fresh orange juice instead.

At meal times go for filled baked potatoes, risottos and stews and pair stir-fries, soups or salads with a carbohydrate for a healthy, well-balanced meal. Good carbohydrates include:

rice and grains

pulses: lentils, beans and dried peas

breakfast cereals: muesli, porridge and wheat blocks, not sugar coated cereals

bread: wholemeal is best but white is still good

pasta

potatoes

noodles

GROUP 2

PROTEIN

The body needs protein for the production of body tissue, so to keep strong and healthy it must be included in your diet. Most people easily consume enough protein so it is not something that you really need to worry about, but it is worth keeping an eye on if you are vegetarian, constantly dieting, or on a very limited budget for food. You don't need to consume a lot but you should make an effort to include a small amount with each meal. Unfortunately a lot of high protein food is also high in fat, so choose lean meat and trim off any fat, and be aware of how much cheese, cream and butter you eat.

The type and quality of protein varies greatly in different foods. Animal proteins such as fish, milk and poultry are the most complete, but there are plenty of good, but not quite as complex plant sources of protein to be found in carbohydrates like grains, pulses, beans and potatoes. The best way to ensure quality, not just quantity, is to try and combine proteins so they complement each other. This is particularly important if you're vegetarian and even more so for vegans who don't eat dairy produce. Try and eat at least two different foods together to obtain a high quality protein; fortunately this is the way that most foods go together anyway – a good example is baked beans on toast which is a very good high fibre, high protein, low-fat snack meal.

Quality high protein foods include:

fish and shell fish   lean meat   poultry   milk   yogurt
----
cheese   eggs   butter   tofu   nuts   seeds   peanut butter
----
seaweed   grains   beans   cereals   pasta

GROUP 3

FRUIT & VEGETABLES

The World Health Organisation recommends that we eat at least 400g, that's almost a pound, or five portions of fruit and vegetables a day – that doesn't include potatoes but does include beans, nuts and seeds. Fruit and vegetables are packed with different vitamins and minerals, so you should try and vary the types you eat and remember that it's impossible to eat too much. Choose fresh or dried fruit in preference to a bar of chocolate or crisps.

The way that you cook the vegetables is of the utmost importance, as it is very easy to destroy the nutrients. Leafy greens are packed with water-soluble vitamin C, so the traditional method of boiling them in water means that when you eat the vegetables, you may still get the fibre but the nutrients and most of the flavour have gone down the drain. Instead try stir-frying, steaming or cooking methods which involve eating the liquid that the vegetables have been cooked in such as soups, stews and pasta sauces.

As soon as they are harvested, fruit and green vegetables begin to deteriorate nutritionally. Don't store them for weeks but eat within a few days of buying. Frozen and canned vegetables are just as good, and in some cases better than fresh. Take frozen spinach for example, which is picked, prepared and quickly frozen within hours, locking in a good percentage of the nutrients.

TOP TIPS FOR EATING WELL

• Base your meals on starchy carbohydrates to get a constant supply of energy.

• Cut back on sugary snacks – don't satisfy your hunger with empty calories that leave you craving more.

• Try to avoid stimulants such as chocolate, cola and coffee – keep your mind and body on an even keel.

• Ensure you get enough high quality protein – try and eat at least 2 together. If you are vegetarian don't base your diet on dairy produce – eat plenty of nuts and pulses.

• Keep an eye on your fat intake, including butter, cream and cheese.

• Try to eat five portions of fruit and vegetables each day – take care when preparing and cooking vegetables, don't destroy their vitamin content.

FOOD SAFETY

The most important thing to remember when you're responsible for feeding yourself, is to keep the kitchen clean. It isn't all that difficult to give yourself (or your house-mates) food poisoning, but if you cook your food carefully and observe basic hygiene and storage rules, you won't put anybody's health at risk.

Here are a few pointers that you should keep in mind:

• Keep the kitchen floor clean, don't encourage mice, rats and other vermin to set up home in your house.

• Don't let dirty pots pile up or bacteria will multiply at an astonishing rate, making your kitchen unsafe and smelly. While you're cooking, try and wash-up as you go and finish off washing the rest straight after you've eaten.

• Wash up in very hot, soapy water. Use rubber gloves and a scrubbing brush and take care to rinse the dishes well with clean hot water.

• Leave the washing-up to air-dry on the draining board – dirty tea towels will just spread germs onto a clean plate, so make sure they're laundered regularly.

• Clean up splashes and spillages immediately after they occur as they make the floor dangerously slippery and can become ingrained and harbour bacteria. Bits of food on the floor and under the cooker can also encourage the odd mouse or two to set up home in your kitchen.

• Wash your hands before you start cooking.

• Keep the fridge clean. It's easy to forget a small lump of cheese that's left to go green at the back of the fridge, if it's not cleaned out regularly. Mould quickly spreads from bad food to healthy like the one bad apple in the sack. It's not only risky but costly.

• Never keep food past its use-by date.

• If a chilled item has been left out of the fridge and has become warm, play safe and throw it away, especially if it's made from dairy produce.

• Store raw meat properly wrapped up and well away from cooked foods. It is better to keep raw meat at the bottom of the fridge so that there's no danger of blood dripping down onto cooked food.

- Use a separate chopping board for raw meat as cont-amination (particularly from pork and poultry) to other foods is common. Scrub boards thoroughly after use.

- Wash your hands thoroughly after touching meat. Take care not to touch pan handles, knives or tea towels whilst preparing raw meat and before you have washed your hands.

- Store dry goods in a cool dark place. Keep bags sealed up with tape and check use-by dates.

- Take chilled or frozen food home as quickly as possible and store at the correct temperature. Don't refreeze food that has defrosted.

- Take care when defrosting food especially meat, fish and poultry. Never force food to defrost quickly but leave it wrapped up at room temperature or even better, in the fridge until completely thawed. Don't ever be tempted by helpful friends who suggest 'rinsing the frozen prawns under the hot tap', or 'leaving the chicken in the sink full of hot water, or in the airing cupboard' to defrost.

- Don't reheat food more than once.

EQUIPMENT

Whether you choose to lodge in college accommodation or a shared house or flat, you'll probably have to share kitchen facilities with a group of other students. This can be a bit of a mixed bag of tricks. No doubt you will argue about whose turn it is to wash-up or empty the bin, but on the plus side, you will have the opportunity to pool resources, not just borrowing the ketchup from your house-mate's cupboard, but sharing kitchen utensils and equipment.

Every High Street has a cheap kitchen shop that's an Aladdin's Cave of useful gadgets from spatulas and can openers to salad spinners and fancy vegetable slicers, so you should be able to get your hands on the essentials listed below. And don't forget that any piece of equipment you buy, is an investment that you'll probably use for years.

ESSENTIALS

- can opener
- cheese grater
- rolling pin
- slotted spoon
- fish slice
- potato masher

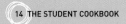

- pastry brush
- 2 chopping boards (1 for raw meat)
- 3 wooden spoons
- metal hand whisk
- metal sieve
- frying pan
- 3 sizes of saucepan with lids
- 2 sizes of bowl
- 1 large sharp knife
- 1 small sharp knife
- set of kitchen scales
- baking sheet (tray)
- roasting tin
- casserole dish with lid

NOT ESSENTIAL BUT VERY HANDY

- garlic press
- vegetable peeler
- measuring jug
- wok

ESSENTIAL INGREDIENTS

If you've only got half a cupboard and a shelf in the fridge to store your provisions, then you're going to have to think carefully about what you buy, or you'll end up with a cupboard packed with pickled gherkins, three varieties of mango chutney, a tub of glacé cherries and no room for your bread or pasta.

Here's a list of all the things you ought to have in store. Apart from the items listed, buy vegetables and salad ingredients to accompany meals, and keep some fresh fruit handy to munch after supper or if you're feeling peckish.

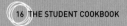

CUPBOARD

ESSENTIALS

- packet of pasta
- packet of long grain rice
- can of chopped plum tomatoes
- can of baked beans
- can of tuna
- small bottle of olive oil
- small bottle of vegetable oil
- bottle of soy sauce
- small bag of lentils
- small tub of dried parsley
- small tub of dried basil
- curry powder
- packet of stock cubes
- tube of tomato purée
- bottle of vinegar
- small packet of flour
- bag of sugar
- salt and pepper

NOT ESSENTIAL, BUT VERY HANDY

- jar of mustard of choice
- bottle of Worcestershire sauce or vegetarian Worcestershire sauce
- can of sweetcorn
- can of corned beef
- can of chickpeas
- can of anchovies in oil
- cornflour
- bottle of tomato ketchup
- jar of honey
- jar of pesto sauce
- cumin seeds
- dried chillies

FREEZER

If you have space in a freezer, then frozen vegetables are very handy; also a loaf of bread and some sausages or chicken pieces (always defrost chicken thoroughly before use).

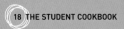

FRIDGE

There are very few chilled items that are real essentials, but there are some that you will use almost everyday. I have not included fresh herbs, as they are something of a luxury for most students, but why not have a go at growing your own – a small pot from the supermarket is not too pricey and with a bit of attention, will survive happily on a sunny windowsill. Alternatively, if you have freezer space, keep a packet of fresh parsley in there, and simply crumble a handful into your cooking as you need it. Other good things to keep in your fridge are a jar of mayonnaise, carton of yogurt or fromage frais, bacon and a jar of curry paste.

ESSENTIALS

• milk

• butter or margarine

• eggs

• Cheese (Cheddar and Parmesan). Cheese adds flavour to your cooking so it's well worth shelling out a little extra for a tangy, mature Cheddar that will really zip up your food rather than opting for the cheaper but blander, mild Cheddars. The same applies to fresh Parmesan. It is expensive, but a little of it, freshly grated, goes a long way. If you're planning to eat plenty of delicious pasta dishes, then the dried, ready-grated variety won't do your cooking any favours as it tends to be lacking in flavour compared to the fresh variety.

POTATOES

There are basically two types of potato, new and old. Although new potatoes are available all year, they are at their best in the spring. Small, waxy and firm they are thin skinned and should be eaten soon after buying. They taste delicious steamed, boiled or stir-fried in olive oil. Old potatoes are thicker skinned and are from the second harvest of the year. They are hardy enough to stand longer lengths of storage and are great for roasting, baking, mashing and making chips.

INTRODUCTION

Don't buy or eat potatoes that have turned green. Cut out any eyes, and sprouting, blackened or bruised areas from the potatoes before you cook them. Store them in a brown paper bag in your food cupboard or some other cool, dark, dry place.

BOILING

If using old potatoes, peel or scrub them well, cutting out all blemishes. Cut into quarters and place in a large saucepan. Cover with cold water, add a pinch of salt and bring to the boil. Simmer for about 20 minutes or so until tender. If you are boiling potatoes for mash, use old ones and cut them into small pieces to speed up cooking time. If you're boiling new potatoes, scrub them well, but don't peel. Put them into salted boiling water and cook for 10–20 minutes depending upon their size, until tender.

BAKING

See Classic Baked Potato on page 26.

ROASTING

Preheat the oven to 190°C, 375°F, Gas 5. Place 3-4 table-spoons of vegetable oil in a roasting tin and put in the oven to heat. Peel the potatoes and cut into quarters, put into the tin with a sprinkle of salt and toss well with the hot oil. Roast for about 1-1½ hours, turning occasionally until crisp on the outside and soft and fluffy on the inside. If you want to speed up the cooking time, boil the potatoes for about 8 minutes before roasting. Add flavour to roast potatoes by cooking them with a couple of whole garlic cloves and a sprig of fresh herbs such as rosemary or sage.

MAKING CHIPS

The best way to cook chips is to fry them twice. If you're going to make your own chips, it's well worth the trouble of doing it properly, as it is the only way to get good crisp chips that are also soft and fluffy inside. Scrub the potatoes in clean cold water and cut into fingers as thick or thin as you like. Wash well, rinsing off any excess starch to stop them sticking together, and dry thoroughly with kitchen paper. Heat a couple of inches of vegetable oil in a small deep frying pan until a cube of bread, when dropped in, turns brown in about a minute. Cook the chips for 5 minutes or until pale golden. Remove with a slotted spoon and drain on kitchen paper. Raise the heat slightly and when the oil is hot enough to brown a cube of bread in 30 seconds, return the chips to the pan for 1-2 minutes until crisp. Drain on kitchen paper and sprinkle with salt.

GARLIC POTATO SOUP

It is important that the garlic is crushed for this recipe – if you don't have a garlic crusher, sprinkle the peeled cloves with a little salt and flatten them under the blade of a heavy knife. If you only have Cheddar in the fridge, you can use it instead.

Heat the butter in a large saucepan and gently cook the garlic and potatoes for 5 minutes until they begin to turn golden. Add the stock, cover and simmer for 20 minutes until the potatoes are cooked and breaking up.

Use a masher to pound the potatoes into the soup – it's very hard to get it completely smooth, so don't worry. Stir in the Tabasco, vinegar and parsley and season to taste.

Ladle into bowls and sprinkle over the cheese. Serve immediately with hot buttered toast or warm crusty bread.

knob of butter or margarine

6 garlic cloves, crushed

500g (1 lb) potatoes, diced

600 ml (1 pint) vegetable stock

few drops Tabasco sauce

1 teaspoon white wine vinegar or lemon juice

1 tablespoon chopped fresh parsley

seasoning

60g (2 oz) feta or mozzarella cheese, thinly sliced

SWEETCORN CHOWDER

500g (1 lb) potatoes, peeled and diced

1 tablespoon vegetable oil

1 onion, chopped

4 rashers streaky bacon, chopped

1 small green chilli, finely chopped

1 red pepper (capsicum), diced

600 ml (1 pint) milk

1 vegetable stock cube

400g (14 oz) can sweetcorn, drained

125g (4 oz) natural fromage frais

seasoning

A chowder is traditionally a thick American soup. It often contains fish, but the name is usually given to any soup that is thickened with potato.

Boil the potatoes in salted, boiling water for 10–15 minutes until tender.

Meanwhile, **heat** the oil in a large pan and fry the onion, bacon, chilli and pepper (capsicum) for 5 minutes until softened. Add the milk and stock cube and simmer gently for 10 minutes.

Mash half the potato until smooth and stir into the soup with the rest of the diced potato and the sweetcorn. Simmer together for 10 minutes. Stir in the fromage frais, season to taste and serve with crusty bread.

 REALLY EASY!

 25 MINUTES

 SERVES 2

LEEK AND POTATO SOUP

A thick, creamy soup of leek and potato with mint and crème fraîche.

Melt the butter in a large saucepan and cook the garlic, chilli, onion, leek and potato for 5 minutes. Pour in the stock, bring to the boil and simmer covered for 30 minutes.

Add the mint, season and cook for a further 10 minutes. Sieve the soup through a metal strainer, working the cooked vegetables through the holes with a wooden spoon.

Return the soup to the pan, stir in the crème fraîche and gently heat through. Serve with warm crusty bread.

REALLY EASY! | 50 MINUTES | SERVES 2 | V

30g (1 oz) butter

1 garlic clove, finely chopped

1 small dried red chilli, crushed

1 small onion, finely chopped

1 large leek, sliced

1 large potato, diced

450 ml ($^3/_4$ pint) vegetable stock

1 tablespoon chopped fresh mint or $^1/_2$ teaspoon dried

seasoning

3 tablespoons crème fraîche or single (pouring) cream

CLASSIC BAKED POTATO

1 very large potato, weighing about 250g (8 oz)

small knob of butter

salt and freshly ground black pepper

Baked potatoes make a great last-resort supper. A piping-hot stuffed potato is cheap, easy and nutritious, and the variety of fillings you can pile into a potato are endless. Choose an old main crop potato such as a King Edward rather than the new, thin-skinned types. For a crunchy skin and floury, fluffy centre leave the potato in the oven for an extra 20 minutes, and for a softer skin, rub a little oil onto the skin before cooking.

Preheat the oven to 200ºC, 400ºF, Gas 6. Scrub the potato in clean, cold water and pat dry.

Pierce the potato a few times with a fork. Place directly onto the oven shelf and bake for an hour until soft. Cut open and serve with butter and a sprinkle of salt and pepper.

REALLY EASY!

1 HOUR

SERVES 1

V

CHEESE AND HAM

Use whatever cheese you have in the fridge
for this recipe.

Split the potato in half and scoop out the flesh to
leave a hollow potato shell about 1 cm ($^1/_2$ inch) thick.
Place the flesh in a bowl with the ham, cheese,
mustard, butter and seasoning and mash well
together.

Pile the filling back into the potato and return to the
oven for 15 minutes until golden.

REALLY EASY! 20 MINUTES SERVES 1

1 hot baked potato

slice of boiled ham, chopped

60g (2 oz) cheese, grated

1 teaspoon English mustard

small knob of butter or margarine

seasoning

POTATO FILLINGS . . .
SOFT CHEESE AND WALNUTS

1 hot baked potato

60g (2 oz) flavoured soft cheese, such as Boursin

1 tablespoon chopped walnuts

Soft cheese is readily available in supermarkets flavoured with garlic, herbs and pepper. With a little heat it melts down to produce a delicious creamy sauce that works brilliantly as a pasta sauce or a topping for a hot potato.

Cut a large cross into the potato and squeeze the potato to open it out. Pop in the soft cheese and sprinkle over the walnuts.

 REALLY EASY!

 3 MINUTES

 SERVES 1

POTATO FILLINGS . . .
MOZZARELLA AND PESTO SAUCE

This recipe is based on the shop-bought, commercial pesto, but if you are using your own, home-made pesto (see recipe on page 90) remember that it's not as strong, so you will need more, but the taste will be well worth the effort.

Cut a large cross into the potato and squeeze the potato to open it out. Mix together the mozzarella, pesto and a little seasoning. Spoon the mixture inside the potato and serve.

1 hot baked potato

60g (2 oz) mozzarella cheese, grated

1 tablespoon pesto sauce

salt and freshly ground black pepper

REALLY EASY!

5 MINUTES

SERVES 1

POTATO FILLINGS . . .
TUNA AND GARLIC MAYONNAISE

1 hot baked potato

125g (4 oz) can of tuna in oil, drained

2 tablespoons garlic mayonnaise

half a red onion or 3 spring onions, chopped

salt and freshly ground black pepper

The wide variety of mayonnaise in the shops is ever increasing. I think garlic mayonnaise goes particularly well with tuna but you could choose lemon, mustard or French.

Cut a large cross into the potato and squeeze the potato to open it out. Mix together the tuna, mayonnaise, onions and season to taste. Spoon the mixture inside the potato and sprinkle over a little black pepper.

 REALLY EASY!

 5 MINUTES

 SERVES 1

POTATO FILLINGS . . .
GARLIC BUTTER

A plain baked potato smothered in garlic butter and served with a crisp green salad makes a simple, tasty supper.

Cut a large cross into the potato and squeeze the potato to open it out. Beat the butter with a wooden spoon to soften it then stir in the garlic, parsley, a little salt and plenty of black pepper. Spoon the mixture inside the potato and serve.

1 hot baked potato

30g (1 oz) butter

2 garlic cloves, crushed or finely chopped

1–2 tablespoons chopped fresh parsley

salt and freshly ground black pepper

 REALLY EASY!

 5 MINUTES

 SERVES 1

POTATO FILLINGS...
MEXICAN STYLE

1 hot baked potato

4 tablespoons
sour cream

1 small avocado, diced

2 tomatoes, skinned
and diced

chilli seasoning

This delicious combination can be used to fill pancakes or piled onto a lettuce-filled pitta.

Cut the potato in half lengthwise and score deeply in a criss-cross pattern with a knife. Spoon over the sour cream and top with avocado and tomato dice. Sprinkle lightly with chilli seasoning and serve.

 REALLY EASY!
 5 MINUTES
 SERVES **1**
 V

FETA AND OLIVE

The tangy combination of feta cheese, olives and lemon juice really gives the potato a lift.

Cut a large cross into the potato and squeeze the potato to open it out. Mix together the feta, chopped olives, oil, lemon juice and seasoning. Spoon the mixture inside the potato and serve.

1 hot baked potato

60g (2 oz) feta cheese, diced

1 tablespoon of pitted black olives, finely chopped

1 tablespoon olive oil

squeeze of lemon juice

seasoning

 REALLY EASY!

 5 MINUTES

 SERVES 1

 V

YOGURT AND CRISPY ONIONS

1 teaspoon vegetable oil

1 small onion, sliced into rings

1 hot baked potato

4–6 tablespoons Greek yogurt

1 tablespoon chopped fresh coriander or parsley

seasoning

Try using fromage frais or soft herb cheese in place of the yogurt.

Heat the oil in a small pan and fry the onions over a high heat for 5–7 minutes until crisp and golden brown. Remove and drain well.

Cut a large cross into the potato and squeeze the potato to open it out. Spoon in the Greek yogurt and top with onion, coriander and a little seasoning.

REALLY EASY! 10 MINUTES SERVES 1 V

BAKED EGG AND CHEDDAR POTATO

Use the scooped out potato flesh for use in another dish such as Bubble and Squeak or Cheese and Chive Potato Cakes.

Slice a lid about 2.5 cm (1 inch) thick off the top of the potato. Scoop out the flesh to leave a shell about 1 cm (1/2 inch) thick.

Season well inside the potato shell then crack the egg and place it carefully inside. Sprinkle over the cheese and replace the lid. Return to the oven for 10 minutes until the egg has set and the cheese has melted.

1 hot baked potato

1 egg

30g (1 oz) Cheddar cheese, grated

seasoning

EASY! 15 MINUTES SERVES 1 V

COTTAGE PIE

500g (1 lb) potatoes, peeled and diced

knob of butter

2 tablespoons milk

seasoning

1 tablespoon vegetable oil

1 onion, finely chopped

250g (8 oz) lean minced beef

1 large carrot, diced

125g (4 oz) frozen peas, thawed

1 tablespoon tomato ketchup

1 teaspoon soy sauce

1/2 teaspoon dried mixed herbs

1 tablespoon chopped fresh parsley

Don't let the college refectory version put you off, as freshly made cottage pie tastes delicious.

Preheat the oven to 200°C, 400°F, Gas 6. Cook the potatoes in boiling water for 10–15 minutes until tender. Drain well and mash with the butter, milk and a little seasoning.

Heat the oil in a pan and fry the onion, mince, carrot and peas for 5 minutes. Add the ketchup, soy sauce, herbs and about 3 tablespoons of water. Cover and simmer gently for 20 minutes.

Check the seasoning and transfer to a deep heatproof dish. Top with the mashed potato and bake for 25 minutes until golden.

EASY!

1 HOUR

SERVES 2

LENTIL SHEPHERD'S PIE

This hearty dish could feed up to 4 people if served with other vegetables on the side, however, on its own it is a complete meal for 2. Keep any leftovers, covered, in the fridge and reheat in the oven the following day.

Heat the oil in a large pan and fry the onion and carrot for 5 minutes until softened. Add the lentils and stock, cover and simmer for 30 minutes until tender.

Meanwhile, **cook** the potatoes in boiling salted water for 10–15 minutes until tender. Drain well and mash with the milk, butter and seasoning.

Preheat the oven to 220°C, 425°F, Gas 7. Stir the tomatoes, peas and parsley into the lentils and simmer together, uncovered, for 10 minutes. Season to taste and spoon into an ovenproof dish. Top with mashed potato and smooth down with the back of a fork. Bake in the oven for 15 minutes until golden brown and heated through.

1 tablespoon vegetable oil

1 onion, finely chopped

1 carrot, finely diced

250g (8 oz) brown or green lentils

450 ml (^{3}/$_4$ pint) vegetable stock

500g (1 lb) potatoes, peeled and cut into chunks

2 tablespoons milk

small knob of butter

seasoning

2 tomatoes, skinned and diced

60g (2 oz) frozen peas

1 tablespoon chopped fresh parsley or 1 teaspoon dried

EASY!

1 HOUR

SERVES 2

V

OCEAN PIE

500g (1 lb) potatoes,
peeled and diced

knob of butter

2 tablespoons milk

seasoning

For The Filling

Large fillet of smoked
haddock or cod weighing
about 250g (8 oz)

60g (2 oz) prawns

30g (1 oz) frozen
peas, thawed

knob of butter

1 tablespoon flour

150 ml (¹/₄ pint) milk

1 tablespoon chopped
fresh parsley

4 tablespoons natural
fromage frais

The fromage frais gives this dish a fresh, slightly sharper flavour than the usual fish pie. If you prefer, use the same quantity of milk instead.

Preheat the oven to 200°C, 400°F, Gas 6. Cook the potatoes in boiling water for 10–15 minutes until tender. Drain well and mash with the butter, milk and a little seasoning.

Meanwhile, **gently** poach the fish fillet in boiling water for 5 minutes. Drain, carefully remove the skin and flake into bite-sized chunks. Arrange the fish, prawns and peas in the base of a deep heatproof dish.

To make the sauce, heat the butter in a small saucepan and when melted, add the flour. Stirring continuously, cook for 1 minute. Gradually add the milk and fromage frais beating until it is all incorporated. Bring to the boil, toss in the parsley and season to taste.

Pour the sauce over the fish and then top with mashed potato. Bake for about 25 minutes until golden. Serve with broccoli or another green vegetable for a hearty supper.

CHEESY POTATO PIE

500g (1 lb) potatoes, peeled and diced

30g (1 oz) butter or margarine

2 tablespoons milk

seasoning

1 tablespoon olive oil

1 onion, chopped

1 large leek, sliced

125g (4 oz) mushrooms, sliced

60g (2 oz) ham, cut into small squares

125g (4 oz) Cheddar cheese, grated

The credit for this recipe goes to a friend of mine who's still at college. She was adamant that I include this invention of hers as she eats it several times a week and it's still her favourite all-in-one meal.

Cook the potatoes in plenty of boiling salted water for 10–15 minutes until tender. Drain them well, return to the pan and mash together with the butter, milk and some seasoning.

Meanwhile, **heat** the oil in a large frying pan and cook the onion, leek and mushrooms together for 5 minutes. Add to the pan of mashed potatoes with the ham and half the cheese. Mix well and check the seasoning.

Transfer the mixture to a heatproof dish, sprinkle over the remaining cheese and place under a hot grill for 3–4 minutes until the cheese is bubbling and golden brown.

REALLY EASY!

30 MINUTES

SERVES 2

SPICY POTATO HOTPOT

If you're short on time, this dish can be finished on top of the stove rather than in the oven.

Preheat the oven to 200ºC, 400ºF, Gas 6. Heat the oil in a large pan and cook the onion, chilli, ginger and garlic for 2–3 minutes. Add the vegetable cubes and cook gently, stirring occasionally, for 10 minutes until they begin to brown.

Blend the cornflour with a little stock and add to the pan with the chilli sauce, lime juice and remaining stock. Bring to the boil, stirring until thickened, then season well to taste.

Transfer to a heatproof casserole dish and bake in the oven for 20 minutes until the vegetables are tender.

 EASY!
 35 MINUTES
 SERVES 2
 V

2 tablespoons vegetable oil

1 small onion, finely chopped

1 small hot chilli, seeded and finely chopped

2.5 cm (1 inch) piece fresh root ginger, finely chopped

2 garlic cloves, finely chopped

1 large potato, diced

2 carrots, diced

2 parsnips, diced

1 teaspoon cornflour

450 ml ($^3/_4$ pint) vegetable stock

1 tablespoon Hot Chilli Sauce (page 251) or a few drops Tabasco sauce

juice of a lime

seasoning

BACON AND TOMATO LAYERED POTATO PIE

knob of butter or margarine

500g (1 lb) potatoes, very thinly sliced

----

1 small onion, thinly sliced

----

2 large tomatoes, thinly sliced

----

8 rashers back bacon, chopped

----

seasoning

----

150 ml (¹/₄ pint) hot chicken stock

A very tasty, inexpensive dish that is great for cold winter evenings.

Preheat the oven to 200°C, 400°F, Gas 6. Generously butter a deep heatproof casserole dish. Layer the potato, onion, tomato and bacon into the casserole dish, seasoning lightly between each layer, finishing with a layer of potato.

Carefully pour over the hot stock, dot with a little butter or margarine, and bake for 45 minutes until the top is lightly browned and the pie is cooked through.

REALLY EASY!

1 HOUR

SERVES 2

ITALIAN POTATO PIE

For the perfect Sunday lunch, serve this melt-in-the-mouth pie with a crisp green salad and a glass of Italian red wine.

Preheat the oven to 220°C, 425°F, Gas 7. Cook the potatoes in plenty of boiling salted water for 15–20 minutes until tender. Drain well and slice thinly.

Arrange a layer of potatoes in a buttered, heatproof dish. Top with a layer of tomatoes sprinkled with onion, oregano and plenty of seasoning, and then a layer of mozzarella. Finish with a layer of potato topped with mozzarella.

Drizzle over the olive oil and bake in the oven for 20 minutes until crisp and golden brown.

500g (1 lb) potatoes, halved

4 tomatoes, skinned and thinly sliced

1 onion, finely chopped

1 teaspoon dried oregano

salt and freshly ground black pepper

150g (5 oz) mozzarella, cheese sliced

4 tablespoons olive oil

REALLY EASY!

50 MINUTES

SERVES 2

V

POTATO CURRY

2 tablespoons
vegetable oil

2 large potatoes, cut into
2.5 cm (1 inch) cubes

1 large onion,
roughly chopped

1 tablespoon hot curry
paste

4 ripe tomatoes, skinned
and quartered

4 garlic cloves, crushed

2 tablespoons chopped
fresh coriander or
parsley

Greek-style yogurt, to
serve (optional)

This tasty curry needs to be served with warm naan bread which can be bought ready-made from most supermarkets.

Heat the oil in a large frying pan and add the potato, onion, curry paste and 2 tablespoons of water. Cover and cook gently for 10–15 minutes, stirring occasionally, until the potato is tender and beginning to brown.

Stir in the tomatoes, garlic and about 5 tablespoons of water, cover and cook for a further 5 minutes until the tomatoes have softened but are still holding their shape. Sprinkle over the coriander and spoon onto plates. Drizzle over the yogurt, if using, and serve with naan bread.

 REALLY EASY!
 30 MINUTES
 SERVES 2
 V

MEDITERRANEAN CHICKEN AND POTATO STEW

This is a cheery one-pot meal that will brighten up a chilly winter evening. Serve it with crusty bread to mop up all the juices.

Heat the oil in a large saucepan, add the chicken, garlic and herbs and quickly fry for 5 minutes, until the chicken is lightly browned all over.

Add about 150 ml (pint) of water or stock, cover and simmer gently for 15 minutes. Add the potatoes and tomatoes and cook for a further 15 minutes until the chicken is cooked through and the potatoes are tender. Season to taste and serve.

REALLY EASY!

 40 MINUTES

 SERVES 2

1 tablespoon olive oil

2 chicken joints

2 garlic cloves, sliced

2 sprigs fresh thyme or $1/2$ teaspoon dried parley

150 ml ($1/4$ pint) water or stock

1 large potato, peeled and cubed

2 ripe tomatoes, chopped

seasoning

SAUSAGE BOMBS

500g (1 lb) potatoes,
peeled and diced

---

knob of butter

---

2 tablespoons milk

---

seasoning

---

6 sausages

---

1 egg, beaten

125g (4 oz) fresh or dried
golden breadcrumbs

---

vegetable oil, for frying

This dish first appeared during war time when it was made with reconstituted dried potato, and known as 'pigs in blankets'!

Cook the potatoes in boiling water for 10–15 minutes until tender. Drain well and mash with the butter, milk and a little seasoning.

Meanwhile **fry** the sausages for around 8 minutes, or until cooked through. Cover each sausage in a coat of mashed potato. Roll in the egg and then in breadcrumbs.

Heat 5 cm (2 inches) of vegetable oil in a frying pan and cook the bombs, three at a time, for 5 minutes or until crisp and golden. Drain on kitchen paper and serve with baked beans or spaghetti hoops.

EASY!

30
MINUTES

SERVES
2

POTATO FLAN WITH MUSHROOMS AND PEPPERS

This makes a delicious change to the usual soggy-bottomed flans as it uses mashed potatoes in place of the pastry.

Cook the potatoes in boiling water for 10–15 minutes until tender. Drain well and mash with the butter, milk and a little seasoning.

Meanwhile, **heat** the oil in a large frying pan, add the pepper (capsicum), onion and mushrooms and cook gently for about 8 minutes until softened and beginning to brown. Season well to taste.

Preheat the oven to 190°C, 375°F, Gas 5. Brush a cake tin or small heatproof dish with oil. Using your fingers press the mashed potato mixture into the tin or dish until the base and sides are evenly covered.

Transfer the vegetables into the potato case. Beat together the milk, egg and a little seasoning. Pour over the vegetables and top with the grated cheese. Bake for 25–35 minutes until set.

500g (1 lb) potatoes, peeled and diced

knob of butter

2 tablespoons milk

seasoning

2 tablespoons vegetable oil

1 red pepper (capsicum), diced

1 small onion, chopped

125g (4 oz) mushrooms, thickly sliced

150 ml ($1/4$ pint) milk

1 egg

60g (2 oz) Cheddar or other hard cheese, grated

 EASY!
 1 HOUR
 SERVES 2
 V

TUNA FISH CAKES

350g (12 oz) potatoes, peeled and diced

1 tablespoon mayonnaise

125g (4 oz) can of tuna in oil, drained

1 tablespoon chopped fresh parsley

1 small onion, finely chopped

seasoning

2 tablespoons flour

1 egg, beaten

8 tablespoons breadcrumbs

vegetable oil, for frying

Canned tuna works incredibly well in fish cakes. Make your own breadcrumbs by coarsely grating stale bread or if you have some handy, the ready-made, dried, golden breadcrumbs will work just as well. If the mixture feels a little too soft, allow it to cool completely before shaping.

Cook the potatoes in plenty of boiling salted water for 10–15 minutes until tender. Drain them well, return to the pan and mash together with the mayonnaise.

Flake the tuna fish and add to the mash with the parsley, chopped onion and season to taste. Mix well together.

With floured hands, shape the mixture into 4 large, flat, even-sized cakes. Dust lightly with flour, then dip into the beaten egg and then the breadcrumbs.

Heat a little oil in a frying pan and gently cook the fish cakes for about 5 minutes on each side until crisp and golden. Remove from the pan with a fish slice and drain on kitchen paper.

REALLY EASY!

30 MINUTES

SERVES 2

CORNED BEEF HASH

Corned beef hash is an amazing dish because it uses few ingredients and yet manages to taste great. Keep a can of corned beef in your cupboard for emergencies and you'll be able to knock up a filling supper in no time.

Cook the potatoes in boiling salted water for 10–15 minutes until tender. Drain well.

Heat the oil in a large frying pan and toss in the potatoes, corned beef, seasoning and Tabasco or hot chilli sauce. Mash together roughly with a fork and leave for 5 minutes so that the base develops a crust. Break up and turn the mixture with the fork and then leave again for a further 5 minutes so that it develops a new crust.

By now, the hash should be heated right through. **Check** the seasoning, adding a little more Tabasco or chilli sauce if liked and divide onto two warm plates. Serve with spaghetti hoops or baked beans for a complete meal.

350g (12 oz) potatoes, unpeeled and diced

2 tablespoons vegetable oil

200g (7 oz) can corned beef, roughly diced

seasoning

few drops Tabasco sauce or Hot Chilli Sauce (page 251)

 REALLY EASY!
 35 MINUTES
 SERVES 2

CHEESE AND CHIVE POTATO CAKES

500g (1 lb) potatoes

60g (2 oz) soft cheese

60g (2 oz) Cheddar cheese, finely diced

2 tablespoons chopped fresh chives

seasoning

2 tablespoons plain flour

1 egg, beaten

90g (3 oz) fresh breadcrumbs

vegetable oil, for frying

The little pieces of cheese melt into the potato and add texture and flavour to these savoury cakes. Use whatever cheese you have in the fridge, mozzarella and Gruyère taste particularly good.

Cook the potatoes in plenty of boiling salted water for 10–15 minutes until tender. Drain well, and mash together with the soft cheese. Stir in the diced Cheddar and chives and season to taste.

With floured hands, shape the mixture into four large, flat, even-sized cakes. Dust lightly with flour, then dip into the beaten egg and then the breadcrumbs.

Heat a little oil in a frying pan and gently cook the potato cakes for about 5 minutes on each side until crisp and golden. Remove from the pan with a palette knife and drain on kitchen paper.

EASY!

30 MINUTES

SERVES **2**

SWEET POTATO STEW

All the vegetables in this stew are naturally sweet-tasting so it makes a really warming, sunny meal. If you can, use orange fleshed sweet potatoes for this recipe, as they look more attractive.

Heat the oil in a large saucepan and cook the sweet potato and carrot for 10 minutes until beginning to brown.

Stir in the sweetcorn and stock, bring to the boil and simmer for 15 minutes until the vegetables are tender. Add the fromage frais and parsley and season to taste. Heat through and serve with crusty bread.

2 tablespoons vegetable oil

500g (1 lb) sweet potatoes, scrubbed and diced

1 large carrot, thickly sliced

250g (8 oz) can sweet-corn, drained

300 ml ($^1/_2$ pint) vegetable stock

150g (5 oz) natural fromage frais

1 tablespoon chopped fresh parsley

seasoning

 REALLY EASY!

 35 MINUTES

 SERVES 2

SAUSAGE, BAKED BEAN AND POTATO HOTPOT

350g (12 oz) potatoes, peeled and halved if large

1 teaspoon vegetable oil

250g (8 oz) sausages, cut into bite-sized pieces

1 large onion, sliced

400g (14 oz) can baked beans

knob of butter or margarine

seasoning

Preheat the oven to 200°C, 400°F, Gas 6. Partially cook the potatoes in salted boiling water for 10 minutes. Drain and set aside to cool slightly.

Meanwhile, **heat** the oil in a large frying pan and cook the sausage pieces for 5 minutes until golden. Remove with a slotted spoon and set aside. Add the onion slices to the same pan and fry over a high heat for 5 minutes until tender and golden. The sausages will have released some of their fat into the pan so it shouldn't be necessary to add any extra oil.

Return the sausage pieces plus the baked beans to the frying pan, heat through and season to taste. Spoon the mixture into a deep casserole dish.

Thinly slice the potatoes and arrange them over the top of the bean mixture, overlapping them. Dot with butter, cover with a lid or foil and bake for 10 minutes. Remove the covering and cook for a further 10 minutes until cooked through and golden-brown around the edges.

REALLY EASY!

40 MINUTES

SERVES 2

POTATOES PROVENÇALE

This French-style dish is easily adapted to make good use of any vegetables you have on hand – try adding canned cannellini beans or frozen peas.

Heat the oil in a frying pan and stir-fry the diced potato and pepper (capsicum) for about 8 minutes until they begin to turn golden brown. Add the onion and garlic and continue to cook for a further 10–12 minutes until all the vegetables are tender and golden brown.

Add the tomatoes, olives, parsley and season to taste. Heat through for 2–3 minutes and serve with a salad.

 REALLY EASY! 25 MINUTES SERVES 2 V

2 tablespoons olive oil

2 large potatoes, diced

1 capsicum, seeded and roughly chopped

1 onion, finely chopped

2 garlic cloves, finely chopped

200g (7 oz) can chopped tomatoes

30g (2 oz) black olives

2 tablespoons chopped fresh parsley or 1 teaspoon dried

salt and freshly ground black pepper

BUBBLE AND SQUEAK

1 large potato, diced

knob of butter

2 large cabbage leaves, roughly chopped

seasoning

Use any sort of leafy green vegetable for this dish, Brussels sprouts and spinach both taste great.

Cook the potato in boiling salted water for 10–15 minutes until tender.

Meanwhile, **heat** the butter in a large frying pan, preferably non-stick, and stir-fry the cabbage with 2 tablespoons of water for about 7 minutes, until softened. Drain the potato well and add to the pan. Mash down roughly with a fork, then leave to cook for about 5 minutes until a crust forms on the bottom.

Break up the mixture and season to taste. Leave to cook for a further 5 minutes so that a crust again forms on the bottom. Slide onto a warm plate and serve with a dollop of tomato ketchup or a dash of Tabasco sauce.

REALLY EASY!

30 MINUTES

SERVES 2

V

CREAMY POTATO GRATIN

Although this gratin takes a long time to cook in the oven, the actual preparation of the dish won't take more than 15 minutes. Serve with a juicy tomato salad for a stylish meal.

Preheat the oven to 180°C, 350°F, Gas 4. Heat the butter in a small pan and cook the mushrooms and garlic for 5 minutes until softened. Strain the liquid from the mushrooms into a jug.

Using a peeler, slice the potatoes into wafer-thin rounds, dropping them straight into a bowl of cold water. Drain the potatoes and pat dry with a clean tea towel.

Mix together the mushroom liquid, cream, milk and plenty of seasoning.

Layer the potatoes, mushrooms and cream in a greased ovenproof dish. Finish with a layer of potatoes and top with cream. Sprinkle over some freshly ground black pepper and bake in the oven for 1 hour until cooked through and crisp and golden on top.

knob of butter

2 large field mushrooms, thinly sliced

2 garlic cloves, finely chopped

3 medium potatoes, peeled

150 ml (¼ pint) carton double (thick) cream

4 tablespoons milk

salt and freshly ground black pepper

 REALLY EASY!
 75 MINUTES
 SERVES 2
 V

POTATO AND CORN BAKE

500g (1 lb) potatoes, diced

60g (2 oz) butter or margarine

125g (4 oz) Cheddar or other cheese, grated

150 ml (¼ pint) milk

3 eggs, beaten

180g (6 oz) drained canned sweetcorn (or use frozen sweetcorn that has been thawed)

seasoning

A creamy potato bake with cheese and sweetcorn.

Preheat the oven to 180ºC, 350ºF, Gas 4. Cook the potatoes in plenty of boiling salted water for 10–15 minutes until tender. Drain well, and mash with the butter, cheese and little of the milk, until completely smooth. Beat in the remaining milk and the eggs.

Stir in the sweetcorn and season generously. Spoon into a greased heatproof dish and bake in the oven for 40 minutes, until set. Serve warm with Hot Chilli Sauce (page 251).

 REALLY EASY!
 1 HOUR
 SERVES 2

BRAISED SPINACH AND LEMONY MASH

You could serve this spinach dish with pasta, rice or bread but it really does taste fantastic on a bed of smooth, lemon-flavoured mashed potatoes. You can use frozen spinach if you wish.

Cook the potatoes in boiling salted water for 10–15 minutes until tender. Drain well and mash with the lemon juice, butter and seasoning until smooth and creamy.

Meanwhile, rinse the spinach leaves briefly in cold water and leave to drain in a colander. Heat the oil in a large frying pan and when it is beginning to sizzle, throw in the garlic, tomatoes and damp spinach. Cover and simmer gently for 8 minutes until the spinach is soft and dark green.

Season the spinach to taste. Spoon the mashed potatoes onto plates, flattening down slightly, and pile the spinach mixture on top. Pour over any juices left in the pan and eat immediately.

500g (1 lb) potatoes

juice of a lemon

knob of butter

seasoning

500g (1 lb) fresh spinach leaves

3 tablespoons olive oil

2 garlic cloves, thinly sliced

3 tomatoes, skinned and roughly chopped

 REALLY EASY!
 20 MINUTES
 SERVES 2

SPANISH TORTILLA

500g (1 lb) new potatoes, scrubbed

2 tablespoons olive oil

1 large red pepper (capsicum), seeded and sliced

1 large onion, sliced

1 garlic clove, crushed

4 eggs, beaten

2 tablespoons milk

1 tablespoon chopped fresh parsley or

1 teaspoon dried

seasoning

Tortillas are delicious eaten hot with green salad but cold leftovers taste great in a sandwich with a dollop of mayonnaise or tomato ketchup. Always use boiled potatoes as the base of the dish but experiment with other ingredients such as spring onions, peas or chopped ham.

Cook the potatoes in boiling water for 10–15 minutes until just tender. Drain and slice.

Heat the oil in a small deep frying pan, preferably non-stick, and gently fry the pepper (capsicum) and onions together for about 8 minutes until very soft and lightly browned. Add the sliced potatoes and the garlic and cook for a further 5 minutes, stirring.

Beat together the eggs, milk, parsley and seasoning. Pour over the vegetables, turn down the heat to the lowest setting and cook gently for 5–8 minutes until the mixture is almost completely set.

Use a spatula to carefully turn the tortilla over or if it's a little tricky, place a plate over the pan, invert the tortilla onto the plate and then slide it back into the pan. Cook for a further 2 or 3 minutes until the underside is golden brown. Cut into wedges and serve.

EASY!

40 MINUTES

SERVES 2

V

ROSTI WITH FRIED EGGS

This is the best ever Sunday brunch. It takes minutes to make and is really filling, but it is fried in oil so don't eat it every day. As a variation try using two medium potatoes and one small carrot. Grate them coarsely and use them as below.

Peel the potatoes and grate coarsely into a bowl. Season with salt and pepper.

Heat a little oil in a frying pan, preferably non-stick. Tip the potatoes into the pan and flatten down with a spatula. Cook over a fairly high heat until crisp and browned underneath. Turn over the rosti and cook for a further 3 minutes until browned on the second side.

Transfer to a warmed plate while you quickly fry the eggs in a little more oil. Top the rosti with the fried eggs and eat straightaway.

2 large potatoes

salt and freshly ground black pepper

vegetable oil for frying

2 eggs

 REALLY EASY!

 15 MINUTES

 SERVES 2

 V

POTATO AND MUSHROOM SALAD

2 cold, boiled potatoes

2 tablespoons olive oil

seasoning

small knob of butter

1 garlic clove, finely chopped

125g (4 oz) button mushrooms

2 tablespoons chopped fresh parsley or basil

1 tablespoon white wine vinegar

1 tablespoon freshly grated Parmesan cheese

This is a tasty way to use up leftover potatoes.
In fact I much prefer them cooked this way to chips.
Try serving on hot buttered toast.

Cut the potatoes into cubes about the same size as the mushrooms. Toss the cubes with 1 tablespoon of oil and season well. Arrange on a baking sheet/tray and place under a preheated grill for 15 minutes, turning occasionally until crisp and golden.

Meanwhile melt the butter in a small saucepan, add the garlic, mushrooms and 2 tablespoons of water, cover and cook gently for 15 minutes. Stir in the parsley and season to taste.

Place the potatoes in a bowl, add the mushrooms with their juices, the remaining oil and wine vinegar. Sprinkle over the Parmesan, toss well together and serve.

REALLY EASY! 35 MINUTES SERVES 1 V

SWEET POTATO AND AUBERGINE SALAD

Chunks of sweet potato, aubergine (eggplant) and peppers (capsicum), roasted with garlic and oil and then tossed with cheese and wine vinegar just before serving.

Preheat the oven to 200°C, 400°F, Gas 6. Place the sweet potato, aubergine (eggplant), garlic cloves and pepper (capsicum) chunks in a roasting tin. Pour over the olive oil and sprinkle with salt. Roast in the oven, turning every quarter of an hour for 45 minutes until crisp and golden on the outside and cooked in the centre.

Turn the hot vegetables with any juices into a serving dish and allow to cool for about 5 minutes. Add the cheese dice and vinegar or lemon juice and toss well together. Check the seasoning and serve warm with garlic bread.

1 large sweet potato, peeled and cut into chunks

1 large aubergine (eggplant), cut into chunks

2 garlic cloves, halved

1 large red or orange pepper (capsicum), cut into 2.5 cm (1 inch) squares

4 tablespoons olive oil

seasoning

125g (4 oz) blue cheese eg Gorgonzola, Dolcellate, Stilton, diced

1 teaspoon wine vinegar or lemon juice

REALLY EASY!

1 HOUR

SERVES 2

V

PASTA

Pasta is simply hard flour blended into a firm dough with water and eggs. It is fairly easy to make fresh pasta yourself but it is time-consuming. When there are so many varieties of pasta you can buy cheaply and cook in a few minutes, opt for dried or ready-made fresh pasta.

INTRODUCTION

DRIED OR FRESH?

There are some people who claim that fresh pasta is superior to the dried. I don't agree, they are both equally good depending upon the sort of dish you want to create. Dried pasta is very cheap, can be stored easily for a long time and is firm with a good bite. If however you fancy a filled pasta such as ravioli or tortellini, there are some very exciting fresh types around such as tomato filled ravioli or tortellini filled with salmon and dill, that are well worth splashing out on for a special occasion. They usually cook in less than 5 minutes and just need tossing with a little warm cream for a super quick, but sophisticated supper.

COOKING

Pasta should be cooked in as a large a pan as possible so that it can move around freely and cook evenly. Bring a large pan of salted water to a rolling boil and toss in the pasta, stir once and cook rapidly until tender with a firm bite. If you're cooking filled pasta shapes, the water should simmer quite gently so that the parcels do not burst open.

MINESTRONE SOUP

1 tablespoon olive oil

4 rashers streaky bacon, chopped

1 small onion, chopped

1 garlic clove, chopped

1 carrot, diced

1 courgette (zucchini), diced

1 small potato, diced

1 celery stick, diced

2 tomatoes, diced

900 ml (1½ pints) vegetable stock

60g (2 oz) pastina

1 tablespoon chopped fresh parsley

seasoning

1 tablespoon freshly grated Parmesan cheese

Don't feel tied to this recipe. Chop and change the vegetables to suit your storecupboard. The word 'minestrone' simply means big soup, but it almost always has pasta in it. Use pastina, tiny pasta shapes specially made for soups, or break strands of spaghetti into very short lengths. For a vegetarian version of this soup simply replace the bacon with 60g (2 oz) chopped mushrooms.

Heat the olive oil in a large saucepan. Fry together the bacon, onion, garlic, carrot, courgette (zucchini), potato and celery for 5 minutes. Add the tomatoes and stock, cover and simmer for 1 hour.

Stir in the pastina and parsley and cook for 10 minutes until the pastina is tender. Check the seasoning, ladle into bowls, sprinkle with Parmesan and serve.

REALLY EASY

90 MINUTES

SERVES **3**

PASTA AND LENTIL SOUP

There's nothing quite as comforting as soup and this one is very tasty and filling on a cold winter's night.

Heat the oil in a large saucepan and cook the celery, onion, garlic and parsley for 5 minutes until softened.

Add the stock, tomato purée, diced potato and tomatoes and the lentils. Bring to the boil and simmer gently for 30 minutes. Add the pasta and cook for a further 10–15 minutes until the lentils and pasta are tender.

Season to taste and divide into bowls. Serve with a swirl of olive oil and a good sprinkling of freshly ground black pepper.

 REALLY EASY!
 75 MINUTES
 SERVES 2
 V

1 tablespoon olive oil, plus extra to serve

2 celery sticks, finely chopped

1 small onion, finely chopped

1 garlic clove, finely chopped

2 tablespoons chopped fresh parsley

1.15 litres (2 pints) vegetable stock

1 tablespoon tomato purée

1 small potato, peeled and diced

2 tomatoes, diced

60g (2 oz) brown or green lentils

60g (2 oz) small pasta shapes

salt and freshly ground black pepper

CHICKEN AND SWEETCORN NOODLE SOUP

1 tablespoon vegetable oil

1 garlic clove, sliced

1 chicken breast, skinned and cut into small pieces

1 tablespoon cornflour

600 ml (1 pint) chicken or vegetable stock

125g (4 oz) sweetcorn kernels

60g (2 oz) vermicelli pasta

1 egg

1 tablespoon fresh lemon juice

seasoning

Chinese-style egg soups such as this one are really easy to make at home. You can substitue chopped-up crab sticks for the chicken but you will only need to fry them for a minute or so.

Heat the oil in a large pan and gently cook the garlic and chicken for 5 minutes until the chicken is white.

Blend the cornflour with a little of the stock and add to the pan with the remaining stock, the sweetcorn, and vermicelli. Bring to the boil, stirring continuously and simmer for 5 minutes.

Beat together the egg and lemon juice and slowly trickle into the pan, stirring with a chopstick or fork to make egg strands. Season to taste and serve the soup immediately.

 REALLY EASY!

 15 MINUTES

 SERVES 2

SPAGHETTI BOLOGNESE

Here is my version of this old favourite. You can use lamb or pork mince in place of beef, if you prefer.

Heat the oil in a saucepan and cook the onion, carrot, garlic and bacon for 5 minutes until softened. Add the mince and cook for a further 5 minutes until the meat has browned. Stir in the chopped tomatoes, purée, and herbs, cover and simmer for 20 minutes.

Meanwhile, **cook** the spaghetti in plenty of boiling, salted water until tender. Drain well and divide into 2 large bowls, making a well in the centre of each. Season the sauce with sugar, salt and pepper and spoon into the spaghetti nests. Serve immediately.

REALLY EASY!

1 HOUR

SERVES **2**

1 tablespoon olive oil

1 onion, chopped

1 carrot, chopped

1 garlic clove, finely chopped

2 rashers streaky bacon, chopped

250g (8 oz) lean minced beef

400g (14 oz) can chopped tomatoes

1 teaspoon tomato purée

1 teaspoon dried mixed herbs

180g (6 oz) spaghetti

pinch of sugar

seasoning

SPAGHETTI ALLA CARBONARA

250g (8 oz) spaghetti

1 tablespoon olive oil

1 garlic clove, finely chopped

1 small onion, chopped

4 slices smoked streaky bacon, roughly chopped

2 eggs, beaten

150 ml (5 fl oz) carton single (pouring) cream

2 tablespoons grated Parmesan cheese

salt and freshly ground black pepper

Vegetarians should use 180g (6 oz) sliced mushrooms in place of the chopped bacon for an equally tasty result.

Cook the pasta in plenty of lightly salted boiling water for 10–12 minutes until tender. Meanwhile heat the oil in a small frying pan and cook the garlic, onion, and bacon for five minutes until golden. Beat together the eggs, cream, half of the Parmesan and a little seasoning.

Drain the pasta well and return to the pan. Quickly add the bacon mixture and the cream mixture and toss well together. Divide into two bowls, sprinkle over the remaining Parmesan and eat immediately.

 REALLY EASY!

 20 MINUTES

 SERVES 2

SPAGHETTI WITH VODKA AND CHILLI

This is a very trendy dish but it really does taste delicious – use extra oil if you don't have any butter but I wouldn't recommend substituting the vodka with any other spirit.

Cook the pasta in plenty of boiling water for 10–12 minutes or until tender.

Meanwhile, **heat** the oil and butter in a small frying pan, add the chillies and tomatoes and cook for 4 minutes. Add the vodka and simmer rapidly for about 3 minutes. Stir in the cream, bring to the boil and remove from the heat. Season to taste.

Drain the pasta well and toss with the sauce. Divide into bowls and serve sprinkled with Parmesan and freshly ground black pepper.

250g (8 oz) spaghetti

1 tablespoon olive oil

small knob of butter

2 small chillies, seeded and finely chopped

2 tomatoes, skinned, seeded and finely chopped

4 tablespoons vodka

4 tablespoons double (thick) cream

salt and freshly ground black pepper

freshly grated Parmesan cheese, to serve

REALLY EASY!

25 MINUTES

SERVES 2

SPAGHETTI MARINARA

2 tablespoons olive oil, plus extra to serve

1 onion, finely chopped

2 garlic cloves, thinly sliced

2 tablespoons roughly torn basil

400g (14 oz) can chopped tomatoes and their juice

250g (8 oz) spaghetti

125g (4 oz) pitted black olives, halved

1 tablespoon capers

salt and freshly ground black pepper

Buy capers pickled in a vinegar from most super-markets. They will keep in the fridge for a quite a while and are great for topping pizzas.

Heat the oil in a saucepan and gently cook the onion, garlic and basil for 5 minutes until softened. Add the tomatoes, cover and simmer for 15 minutes.

Meanwhile **cook** the pasta in plenty of boiling, salted water for 10–12 minutes or until tender.

Add the olives and capers to the tomatoes and season to taste. Drain the pasta and return to the pan. Add about half of the sauce to the pasta and toss well together to mix.

Divide into 2 serving bowls and spoon the remaining sauce over the pasta. Drizzle with a little extra olive oil and sprinkle with some freshly ground black pepper. Eat immediately.

REALLY EASY!

35 MINUTES

SERVES 2

V

GARLIC OIL SPAGHETTI

This is strictly for true garlic fans. If you wish, add a sliced fresh or small dry chilli with the garlic.

Cook the pasta in plenty of boiling water for 10–12 minutes or until tender.

Meanwhile **heat** the oil in a small saucepan. Add the garlic and fry gently for 3–4 minutes, until golden, taking care not to burn the garlic. Remove the garlic.

Drain the pasta and return to the pan. Add the flavoured oil and toss well together. Season generously adding a little hot water or more oil if the pasta seems dry. Serve immediately.

250g (8 oz) spaghetti

4 tablespoons olive oil

6 garlic cloves, thickly sliced

salt and freshly ground black pepper

REALLY EASY!

20 MINUTES

SERVES **2**

V

SPAGHETTI WITH ANCHOVIES, GARLIC AND CHILLI

This is my all time favourite pasta dish. My mum always cooks it for me when I visit and I make it myself for friends at least once a week. For a more creamy consistency, after cooking the garlic, crush it with a heavy knife and whisk it back into the sauce.

Place a big pan of salted water on to boil. In a small saucepan heat the olive oil and gently cook the garlic and chilli pieces until golden and crisp. Be careful not to burn the garlic. Remove with a slotted spoon and set aside.

When the water is boiling, add in the pasta and cook until tender. Meanwhile add the can of anchovies, including the oil to the saucepan and cook for about 2 minutes. Now add 150 ml (¼ pint) of water and boil gently until the pasta is ready, whisking with a fork to break up the anchovies.

Drain the pasta well and return to the pan. Pour over the sauce and toss together. If it is too dry, add a little more olive oil or a couple of tablespoons of hot water. Divide between 2 bowls and sprinkle over plenty of black pepper. Sprinkle with the reserved garlic, and chilli if you wish.

4 tablespoons olive oil

4 garlic cloves, halved

1 red chilli, quartered

250g (8 oz) spaghetti

small can of anchovies in olive oil

freshly ground black pepper

EASY!

20 MINUTES

SERVES **2**

CRAIG'S MACARONI CHEESE

250g (8 oz) macaroni

30g (1 oz) butter or margarine

1 small onion, chopped

1 garlic clove, crushed

30g (1 oz) flour

300ml (1/2 pint) milk

180g (6 oz) mature Cheddar cheese, grated

1 tablespoon wholegrain mustard

seasoning

Macaroni cheese is a student classic as it's so filling and simple to make. When I first met eternal student Craig, he cooked me this every single time I went round for supper. Fortunately, I've taught him a thing or two since!

Cook the pasta in plenty of boiling salted water until tender. Meanwhile, heat the butter in a saucepan and gently cook the onion and garlic for 5 minutes until softened.

Stir the flour into the pan and blend into the butter and onions with a wooden spoon. Gradually beat in the milk to make a smooth sauce. If it does become lumpy, whisk it vigorously.

Bring gently to the boil and add 125g (4 oz) of the cheese and the mustard. Heat gently for a couple of minutes, until the cheese melts and season to taste.

Drain the pasta and return to the pan. Pour in the sauce and mix well, then transfer to a heatproof dish, scatter over the remaining cheese and pop under a preheated grill for 5 minutes until golden and bubbling.

 REALLY EASY!
 30 MINUTES
 SERVES 2
 V

MACARONI WITH BROCCOLI AND BLUE CHEESE

Pre-packed broccoli in supermarkets can often be quite expensive, so if you are near any market stalls, always check out the price – you'll find it is often cheaper and you can buy the exact amount you want.

Cook the pasta in plenty of lightly salted boiling water for 7 minutes. Add the broccoli to the pan and cook together for a further 5 minutes until both pasta and broccoli are tender.

Meanwhile, **heat** the butter in a small pan, add the flour and beat together with a wooden spoon until smooth. Gradually stir in the stock, bring to the boil and season to taste. Add the lemon juice and rind and simmer gently for 1 minute.

Drain the pasta and broccoli. Put in a dish and pour over the sauce. Sprinkle over the blue cheese and toss well together and serve.

180g (6 oz) macaroni

250g (8 oz) broccoli florets

knob of butter or margarine

1 tablespoon flour

200 ml (7 fl oz) vegetable stock

seasoning

grated rind and juice of half a lemon

60g (2 oz) blue cheese, crumbled

 REALLY EASY! 20 MINUTES SERVES 2 V

ROSY SPIRALS

250g (8 oz) pasta spirals

500g (1lb) carton creamed tomatoes

90g (3 oz) pack garlic and herb flavoured soft cheese, e.g. Boursin

1/2 teaspoon sugar

salt and freshly ground black pepper

1 tablespoon chopped fresh parsley

You will find cartons of creamed or sieved tomatoes in any supermarket, usually positioned near the tomato purée. Or if you have a 400g (14 oz) can of chopped tomatoes handy, pass through a sieve and use instead.

Cook the pasta in plenty of boiling water for 10–12 minutes or until tender.

Meanwhile, **place** the creamed tomatoes and soft cheese and sugar in a small saucepan. Heat together gently for 5–6 minutes, stirring until the cheese has melted and the sauce has warmed through. Season to taste and stir in the parsley.

Drain the pasta well and toss together with the sauce. Divide into bowls and serve with a sprinkling of freshly ground black pepper.

REALLY EASY! | 20 MINUTES | SERVES 2 | V

CREAMY MUSHROOM PASTA

Always use double (thick) cream for this recipe as you can boil it without fear of it curdling.

Cook the pasta in plenty of boiling water for 10–12 minutes or until tender.

Meanwhile, **heat** the butter in a small saucepan and gently cook the garlic and mushrooms for 5 minutes. Add the cream, parsley and season to taste. Bring to the boil and simmer gently for 3 minutes.

Drain the pasta well and toss together with the sauce. Divide into serving bowls and sprinkle over the Parmesan. Serve immediately.

250g (8 oz) pasta shapes

small knob of butter or margarine

1 large garlic clove, finely chopped

180g (6 oz) large flat mushrooms, sliced

150 ml (¼ pint) double (thick) cream

1 tablespoon chopped fresh parsley

seasoning

1 tablespoon freshly grated Parmesan cheese

HAZELNUT PASTA

250g (8 oz) pasta shapes

4 tablespoons olive oil

2 garlic cloves,
roughly chopped

125g (4 oz) hazelnuts,
roughly chopped

3 tablespoons freshly
grated Parmesan cheese

seasoning

A lovely pasta dish flavoured with garlic, parmesan and hazelnuts.

Cook the pasta in plenty of boiling water for 10–12 minutes or until tender.

Meanwhile, **heat** the oil in small frying pan and gently cook the garlic and hazelnuts for about 5 minutes until lightly golden.

Drain the pasta well and toss with the hazelnut mixture, Parmesan and plenty of seasoning. Serve immediately.

REALLY EASY!

 20 MINUTES

SERVES 2

PASTA ALFREDO

One of the fastest pasta dishes you can make – great when you're really hungry.

Cook the pasta in plenty of salted boiling water for 10–12 minutes or until tender.

Beat together the cream, egg, Parmesan and plenty of seasoning. Drain the pasta well and return to the pan. Add the cream mixture and butter and toss well together. Divide into bowls and serve immediately with a little extra Parmesan sprinkled over.

250g (8 oz) tagliatelle

4 tablespoons double (thick) cream

1 egg

2 tablespoons freshly grated Parmesan cheese, plus extra to serve

salt and freshly ground pepper

60g (2 oz) butter, cut into small pieces

FARFALLE FLORENTINA

2 tablespoons olive oil

1 small onion,
finely chopped

2 garlic cloves,
finely chopped

1 small hot chilli,
chopped (optional)

400g (14 oz) can of
chopped tomatoes

1 teaspoon honey
or sugar

1 tablespoon chopped
fresh parsley or
1 teaspoon dried

seasoning

250g (8 oz) farfalle
(pasta bows)

250g (8 oz) spinach,
thawed if frozen

125g (4 oz) mozzarella
cheese, sliced

1 tablespoon freshly
grated Parmesan cheese

If you ever see Florentine or Florentina on a menu, it means the dish originates from Florence in Italy – although there's no guarantee that it's true, you can be sure that the dish will contain spinach and usually cheese.

Place a large saucepan of salted water on to boil. Heat 1 tablespoon of the oil in a small saucepan and gently fry the onion, garlic and chilli, if using, for 5 minutes until softened. Stir in the tomatoes, honey and parsley, season to taste, cover and simmer for 10 minutes.

Cook the pasta bows for 10–12 minutes until tender. Meanwhile, if using fresh spinach, cook it in a little boiling water for 5 minutes, until wilted. Drain the spinach well and stir into the tomato sauce – if using frozen spinach, you won't need to cook it, just stir it directly into the sauce.

Drain the pasta and return to the pan, pour over the sauce and toss well together. Turn into a heatproof dish and sprinkle over the mozzarella, Parmesan and remaining tablespoon of olive oil. Place under a preheated grill for 5 minutes until the cheese is bubbling and golden.

EASY!

35 MINUTES

SERVES **2**

V

PASTA WITH WALNUTS AND CORIANDER

250g (8 oz) pasta

1 tablespoon olive oil

125g (4 oz) cream cheese

60g (2 oz) Gruyère or Cheddar cheese

60g (2 oz) chopped walnuts

2 tablespoons chopped fresh coriander plus extra to serve

salt and freshly ground black pepper

This creamy dish is amazingly quick and easy to prepare. Add a bit of variety to it by experimenting with different nuts such as hazelnuts, almonds or even peanuts.

Cook the pasta in plenty of lightly salted boiling water for about 12 minutes, or until tender.

Meanwhile, **beat** together the olive oil, cream cheese, Gruyère, walnuts, coriander and plenty of seasoning.

Drain the pasta, toss in the cheese mixture and mix well together for 1 or 2 minutes until the cheese melts and coats the pasta. Divide into 2 bowls and serve with a sprinkling of black pepper and coriander.

REALLY EASY! **15** MINUTES SERVES **2**

BROCCOLI PASTA

All parts of broccoli are edible – peel the juicy stalk with a potato peeler or sharp knife and slice into thin rounds.

Cook the pasta in plenty of salted boiling water for 8 minutes. Add the broccoli to the pan and cook for a further 4 minutes until the pasta and vegetables are tender.

Meanwhile, **heat** the oil in a small frying pan and gently cook the garlic, onion, chilli for 5 minutes until softened. Season to taste.

Drain the pasta well and toss with the onion mixture. Divide into serving bowls and sprinkle with Parmesan. Serve immediately.

180g (6 oz) pasta shapes eg bows, shells

180g (6 oz) broccoli, cut into small florets

4 tablespoons olive oil

2 garlic cloves, thinly sliced

1 red onion, finely chopped

1 small red chilli, seeded and finely chopped

seasoning

2 tablespoons freshly grated Parmesan cheese

REALLY EASY!

 15 MINUTES

 SERVES 2

PASTA PRIMAVERA

2 tomatoes, quartered

3 tablespoons olive oil

1 onion, sliced

1 garlic clove, finely chopped

180g (6 oz) pasta shapes

125g (4 oz) frozen peas

1 courgette (zucchini), sliced

2 tablespoons chopped fresh parsley

Primavera means spring and this dish is traditionally made with spring vegetables such as asparagus, courgettes (zucchini) and fresh peas.

Place a big pan of salted water onto the boil. Arrange the tomatoes skin side up on a baking sheet/tray and brush with a little of the olive oil. Cook for about 8 minutes under a preheated grill, turning once, until golden brown and a little charred.

While the tomatoes are grilling, heat the remaining oil in a saucepan and gently cook the onion and garlic for 10 minutes until softened and lightly golden.

Cook the pasta for 10–12 minutes or until tender. Meanwhile, add the grilled tomatoes, peas and courgettes (zucchinis) to the pan of onions. Season well, cover and cook gently for 5–10 minutes.

Drain the pasta well and toss with the vegetables and parsley. Serve immediately.

 EASY!

 40 MINUTES

 SERVES 2

PASTA NAPOLITANA

This is a classic tomato sauce. It tastes really good simply tossed with spaghetti and served with a sprinkling of Parmesan.

To make the sauce, heat the oil in a saucepan and gently cook the onion and garlic for 5 minutes until softened. Add the tomatoes, purée, oregano, sugar and seasoning. Bring to the boil and simmer very gently, uncovered for about 30 minutes until thick and pulpy.

Meanwhile **cook** the pasta in plenty of boiling salted water for 10–12 minutes or until tender. Drain and return to the pan. Add about half of the sauce to the pasta and toss well together to mix.

Divide into 2 serving bowls and spoon the remaining sauce over the pasta. Sprinkle with Parmesan and serve immediately.

EASY!

45 MINUTES

SERVES 2

V

2 tablespoons olive oil

1 onion, finely chopped

2 garlic cloves, finely chopped

400g (14 oz) can chopped tomatoes, and their juice

1 tablespoon tomato purée

1 teaspoon dried oregano

pinch of sugar

seasoning

250g (8 oz) pasta

1 tablespoon freshly grated Parmesan cheese, to serve

THREE-CHEESE SAUCE WITH PISTACHIOS

125 ml (4 fl oz) single cream

45g (1 1/2 oz) Gorgonzola cheese, crumbled

45g (1 1/2 oz) grated fresh Parmesan cheese

30g (1 oz) grated Gruyère cheese

30g (1 oz) shelled pistachio nuts, chopped

1 teaspoon finely chopped basil

ground white pepper

180g (6 oz) pasta, cooked

This is a sauce recipe to serve over any pasta of your choice. To save buying large pieces of cheese, look out for individual packs in the 'Pick and Mix' sections of some supermarkets.

Put the cream into a saucepan and bring slowly to the boil. Reduce the heat, add the Gorgonzola cheese and stir until melted and smooth. Stir in the Parmesan and Gruyère cheeses. Cook over a low heat, stirring constantly, until the sauce is thick and smooth.

Add the pistachio nuts and basil. Season to taste with the white pepper. To serve, pour over hot cooked pasta of your choice.

 REALLY EASY!
 10 MINUTES
 SERVES 2
 V

PENNE WITH PEPPERS

A very quick and filling dish of pasta with red peppers (capsicum), garlic, basil and Parmesan.

Heat the oil in a large frying pan and cook the peppers (capsicum) over a medium heat for at least 10 minutes until very soft. When you begin to cook them, they will steam as all the natural waters are released. The steaming subsides and the peppers (capsicum) turn a lovely caramel colour when they are ready.

Meanwhile, **cook** the pasta in plenty of boiling salted water until tender. Drain well and add to the frying pan. Toss in the herbs, Parmesan and plenty of seasoning. Mix well together, spoon into bowls and eat immediately.

4 tablespoons olive oil

2 large red peppers (capsicum) cut into strips

250g (8oz) penne (pasta quills)

big handful fresh basil or parsley, roughly chopped

2 tablespoons freshly grated Parmesan cheese

salt and freshly ground black pepper

REALLY EASY!

15 MINUTES

SERVES 2

TAGLIATELLE WITH MEATBALLS

250g (8 oz) minced beef

60g (2 oz) fresh white breadcrumbs

1 tablespoon freshly grated Parmesan cheese, plus extra to serve

1 egg, beaten

1 tablespoon chopped fresh parsley

seasoning

1 tablespoon olive oil

1 small onion, chopped

1 garlic clove, chopped

400g (14 oz) can chopped tomatoes

1 tablespoon chopped fresh basil or 1 teaspoon dried

250g (8 oz) tagliatelle

Tiny meatballs in a tomato sauce served on pasta nests.

Place the minced beef, breadcrumbs, Parmesan, egg, parsley and a little seasoning in a bowl and mix together. Shape into about 12 small balls.

Heat the olive oil in a large saucepan and cook the onion, garlic and meatballs for 5 minutes until the meatballs are browned all over. Add the tomatoes and basil and season to taste. Simmer, covered, for about 20 minutes.

Meanwhile, **cook** the tagliatelle in plenty of boiling salted water until tender. Drain well and divide into 2 large bowls, making a well in the centre of each. Spoon the meatballs and tomato sauce into the pasta nests and serve sprinkled with a little extra Parmesan.

 EASY!

 30 MINUTES

 SERVES **2**

PASTA WITH MUSHROOM SAUCE

This is really a cheats' dish but if you're pushed for time, you can turn out a hearty meal with very little effort.

Place a large saucepan of salted water on to boil. Heat the oil in a small saucepan and gently fry the onion, garlic and bacon for 5 minutes, until softened.

Add the mushrooms and cook for a further 2 minutes. Stir in the soup, season to taste and simmer for 10 minutes, or until the pasta is ready.

Cook the pasta for 10–12 minutes until tender. Drain well and divide into two bowls. Stir the parsley into the sauce and pour over the pasta. Serve immediately with a good sprinkling of black pepper and freshly grated Parmesan.

REALLY EASY!   20 MINUTES   SERVES 2

1 tablespoon olive oil

1 small onion, finely chopped

1 garlic clove, finely chopped

2 rashers streaky bacon, chopped

125g (4 oz) mushrooms, sliced

150 ml (1/4 pint) can of condensed cream of mushroom soup

seasoning

1 tablespoon chopped fresh parsley

250g (8 oz) tagliatelle

1 tablespoon freshly grated Parmesan, to serve (optional)

TAGLIATELLE WITH PESTO SAUCE

2 handfuls fresh
basil leaves

2 tablespoons pine nuts

2 garlic cloves

2 tablespoons olive oil

60g (2 oz) butter

60g (2 oz) freshly
grated Parmesan cheese

250g (8 oz) tagliatelle

seasoning

If you're lucky enough to have a mini food processor, it will make short work of blending together the basil, pine nuts and garlic.

Place a big pan of salted water on to boil. Use a heavy knife to finely chop together the basil, pine nuts and garlic cloves until blended. Place the mixture in a small bowl and stir in the oil, butter and Parmesan.

When the water is boiling, toss in the pasta and cook until tender. Scoop out 2 tablespoons of hot water from the pasta pan and add to the pesto mixture. Drain the pasta and return to the pan.

Add the pesto and toss well together until thoroughly mixed. Season to taste and serve immediately with a little extra Parmesan scattered on top.

EASY!

20 MINUTES

SERVES 2

V

PASTA WITH CREAMY PRAWNS

Spaghetti in a creamy, tomato sauce with prawns.

Cook the pasta in plenty of boiling salted water until tender.

Meanwhile, **place** the cream, tomato ketchup, dill, garlic and prawns together in a small saucepan. Heat gently and slowly bring to the boil. Remove from the heat and season to taste.

Drain the pasta well and return to the pan. Add the prawn sauce and toss with the pasta to coat. Turn into bowls and serve at once.

REALLY EASY!

15 MINUTES

SERVES 2

250g (8 oz) spaghetti or tagliatelle

150 ml (1¼ pint) double cream

1 tablespoon tomato ketchup

1 teaspoon dried dill

1 garlic clove, finely chopped

125g (4 oz) large, cooked, peeled prawns

seasoning

PASTA WITH TUNA AND MUSHROOMS

250g (8 oz) pasta shapes

1 onion, chopped

1 garlic clove, sliced

1 tablespoon olive oil

200g (7oz) can tuna in oil, drained

180g (6 oz) button mushrooms, sliced

2 tablespoons chopped fresh parsley

salt and freshly ground black pepper

Cook the pasta in plenty of boiling salted water until tender. Meanwhile fry the onion and garlic in the oil for 5 minutes until softened.

Add the tuna and mushrooms and 150ml ($^1/_4$ pint) of water and cook gently for 10 minutes or until the pasta is cooked. Stir in the parsley and season to taste.

Drain the pasta and return to the pan. Tip in the sauce and toss well together. Divide into bowls and serve with a good sprinkling of black pepper on each.

REALLY EASY!

30 MINUTES

SERVES 1

PASTA FAGOLI

This is a traditional Southern Italian dish – 'fagoli' meaning beans.

Heat the oil in a large saucepan and cook the onion and garlic for 5 minutes until softened.

Add the stock, beans and tomatoes and simmer together for 10 minutes. Add the pasta and cook for a further 10–15 minutes until tender.

Stir in the parsley and season to taste. Serve immediately.

2 tablespoons olive oil

1 onion, roughly chopped

2 garlic cloves, finely chopped

600 ml (1 pint) vegetable stock

400g (14 oz) can cannellini beans, drained

200g (7 oz) can chopped tomatoes, drained

125g (4 oz) small pasta shapes

4 tablespoons chopped fresh parsley

seasoning

PASTA OMELETTE

1 tablespoon olive oil

1 garlic clove, sliced

60g (2 oz) cooked pasta shapes

2 eggs

2 tablespoons milk

1 tablespoon chopped fresh parsley or 1 teaspoon dried

seasoning

30g (1 oz) Cheddar cheese, grated

This is a great way of using leftover pasta – even pasta that has been coated in a tomato or cheese sauce works well in an omelette. Serve with salad or baked beans for a complete meal.

Heat the oil in a small frying pan and stir-fry the garlic and pasta for 3–4 minutes until heated through.

Beat together the eggs, milk, parsley and a little seasoning. Pour over the pasta and cook gently for 3–4 minutes until the egg is almost set on top and golden brown underneath.

Sprinkle over the cheese and place under a hot grill for 2–3 minutes until golden and bubbling. Slide onto a plate and serve immediately.

REALLY EASY!

15 MINUTES

SERVES 1

V

CHEESY PASTA PUFF

This cheese soufflé is another great way of using up leftover pasta.

Cook the pasta in plenty of boiling water for 10–12 minutes or until tender. Drain well and set aside to cool. Preheat the oven to 180°C, 350°F, Gas 4.

Melt the butter in a saucepan, add the flour and cook, stirring, for 1 minute. Gradually beat in the milk to make a smooth sauce. Stir in the mustard, Cheddar and plenty of seasoning. Bring to the boil, stirring until the cheese melts. Set aside for 5 minutes to cool.

Stir the pasta and egg yolks into the sauce. In a separate bowl, whisk the egg whites until stiff and carefully fold into the pasta mixture.

Spoon into a greased heatproof dish and sprinkle over the Parmesan. Bake in the oven for 40–45 minutes until puffed and golden brown. If the topping browns too quickly, cover with foil. Serve immediately with a crisp green salad.

180g (6 oz) macaroni or other small pasta shapes

60g (2 oz) butter or margarine

60g (2 oz) plain flour

300 ml ($^{1}/_{2}$ pint) milk

1 teaspoon English mustard

125g (4 oz) Cheddar cheese, grated

seasoning

3 eggs, separated

1 tablespoon freshly grated Parmesan cheese

 EASY!
 1 HOUR
 SERVES 2
 V

PASTA WITH TOMATO AND MOZZARELLA

4 large ripe tomatoes, halved

1 large onion, cut into 8 wedges

3 tablespoons olive oil

1 garlic clove, finely chopped

4 basil leaves, roughly chopped

seasoning

250g (8 oz) pasta

125g (4 oz) mozzarella, cut into small dice

This is a perfect summertime recipe which makes the most of the abundance of plump red tomatoes.

Place the tomatoes skin side up with the onions on a baking sheet/tray and drizzle over 2 tablespoons of the olive oil. Cook for about 8 minutes under a preheated grill, turning once, until golden brown and a little charred.

Heat the remaining oil in a small saucepan and fry the garlic for 2 minutes. Add the tomato mixture and the basil and season well to taste. Cover and simmer gently for 10 minutes or until pasta is ready.

Cook the pasta in plenty of boiling salted water until tender. Drain well and return to the pan. Toss in the sauce and mix well together. Sprinkle over the mozzarella and mix again, turn into bowls and serve immediately.

EASY! **25** MINUTES SERVES **2** V

RIGATONI WITH AUBERGINES

A pasta sauce made with vegetable chunks is best paired with large pasta shapes such as rigatoni (tubes), shells or quills rather than ribbons.

Cook the pasta in plenty of boiling water for 10–12 minutes or until tender.

Meanwhile, **cut** the aubergine (eggplant) into sticks about 2.5 cm (1 inch) long and 5 mm ($^1/_4$ inch) thick. Heat the oil in a large frying pan and stir-fry the aubergine (eggplant) and garlic for 7 minutes until softened and golden.

Drain the pasta well and add to the frying pan. Stir in the herbs, Parmesan and plenty of seasoning. Divide into bowls and serve immediately with a little extra Parmesan sprinkled over.

250g (8 oz) pasta tubes

1 large aubergine (eggplant) weighing around 350g (12 oz)

5 tablespoons olive oil

2 garlic cloves, sliced

big handful fresh basil or parsley, roughly chopped

3 tablespoons freshly grated Parmesan cheese, plus extra to serve

salt and freshly ground black pepper

 REALLY EASY!
 20 MINUTES
 SERVES 2
 V

PASTA SPIRALS WITH BUTTERY COURGETTES

2 small courgettes (zucchini)

30g (1 oz) butter

1 tablespoon olive oil

2 garlic cloves, finely chopped

1/2 teaspoon dried rosemary

250g (8 oz) pasta spirals

seasoning

1 tablespoon freshly grated Parmesan cheese

Pasta spirals tossed with tender courgette (zucchini) sticks and served with Parmesan.

Slice each courgette (zucchini) lengthwise into four strips. Place the strips on top of each other and slice lengthwise into thin sticks. Cut them widthways to make small sticks.

Heat the butter and oil together and cook the garlic, courgettes (zucchini) and rosemary over a fairly high heat for about 7–8 minutes until the courgettes (zucchini) are golden brown. Season to taste.

Meanwhile **cook** the pasta in plenty of boiling salted water until tender. Drain well and return to the pan. Add the courgette (zucchini) mixture and toss together. Divide into serving dishes and sprinkle over the Parmesan.

 REALLY EASY!
 15 MINUTES
 SERVES 2
 V

BAKED PEPPER PASTA

Grilled peppers (capsicum) tossed with pasta, tomatoes, herbs and mozzarella.

Preheat the oven to 200°C, 400°F, Gas 6. Cook the pasta in plenty of boiling salted water for 10–12 minutes or until tender. Drain.

Meanwhile, **brush** the peppers (capsicum) with oil and place under a preheated grill for 8 minutes, turning once, until tender. Cut into bite-size pieces.

Toss together the pasta, peppers (capsicum), garlic, basil, tomatoes and mozzarella. Season to taste and spoon into a greased ovenproof dish. Sprinkle with the Parmesan and bake in the oven for 15–20 minutes until heated through and golden brown on top.

REALLY EASY! | 40 MINUTES | SERVES 2 | V

250g (8 oz) pasta shapes

1 large red pepper (capsicum), seeded and quartered

1 large orange pepper (capsicum), seeded and quartered

1 tablespoon olive oil

2 garlic cloves, finely chopped

2 tablespoon roughly chopped fresh basil or 1 teaspoon dried

400g (14 oz) can chopped tomatoes, drained

150g (5 oz) mozzarella cheese, diced

seasoning

2 tablespoons freshly grated Parmesan cheese

CAULIFLOWER PASTA WITH CRISPY CRUMBS

It is very important to use large pasta shapes in this recipe. The big tubes (rigatoni) are particularly good. A different, but very delicious way to eat cauliflower.

Place a big pan of salted water on to boil. Heat the oil in a small pan and fry the onion and garlic together for 5 minutes until softened. Add the tomatoes and parsley and season to taste. Cover and simmer very gently until the pasta is ready.

Toss the cauliflower and pasta into the pan of boiling water and cook together for around 12 minutes until the pasta is tender and the cauliflower is soft.

Meanwhile make the topping. **Heat** the remaining oil in a frying pan, add the breadcrumbs and stir-fry for 5 minutes or so, until crisp and golden brown.

Drain the pasta and cauliflower well and return to the pan. Stir in the tomato sauce and mix thoroughly together. The cauliflower will break up and blend with the tomato sauce. Divide into serving bowls and sprinkle over the crispy crumbs. Serve straightaway.

EASY! · 25 MINUTES · SERVES 2 · V

1 tablespoon olive oil

1 small onion, chopped

2 garlic cloves, finely chopped

200g (7 oz) can chopped tomatoes

1 tablespoon chopped fresh parsley or 1 teaspoon dried

seasoning

1 small cauliflower, cut into florets

180g (6 oz) large pasta tubes, shells or bows

For The Topping

1 tablespoon olive oil

4 tablespoons fresh white breadcrumbs

PASTA AND AUBERGINE LAYER

250g (8 oz) pasta shapes

1 large aubergine (eggplant)

1 tablespoon olive oil

400g (14 oz) can of chopped tomatoes

1 teaspoon dried basil

salt and freshly ground black pepper

125g (4 oz) mozzarella cheese, grated

1 tablespoon grated Parmesan cheese

This recipe not only tastes delicious but also looks quite impressive. It's a perfect supper dish if you're entertaining, and if you feel like splashing out, use a handful of fresh basil leaves in place of the dried.

Preheat the oven to 200ºC, 400ºF, Gas 6. Cook the pasta in plenty of lightly salted boiling water for about 12 minutes or until just tender.

Meanwhile, **slice** the aubergine (eggplant) into thick rounds, brush with the olive oil and sprinkle lightly with a little salt. Place under a preheated grill for 6–8 minutes until golden brown on both sides and soft in the centre.

Drain the pasta well and return to the pan. Add the can of tomatoes and basil, mix to combine and season to taste.

Spoon one-third of the pasta mixture into the base of a heatproof dish. Arrange half of the aubergine (eggplant) slices on top of the pasta and sprinkle over half of the mozzarella. Repeat to make a second layer, finishing with the final third of pasta.

Sprinkle over the Parmesan, and bake for 15–20 minutes until the pasta has a golden brown crust and is piping hot. If the top browns too quickly, cover with a lid or foil.

 EASY!

 40 MINUTES

 SERVES **2**

RICE
AND
GRAINS

Cheap, nutritious and very easy to cook, rice is the staple diet in many countries. It thrives on waterlogged, marshy soil where other cereals, such as wheat will not grow.

INTRODUCTION

Although there are literally hundreds of different types of rice, there are only two basic grains, long and short. Short rice is stirred during cooking to release the starch and produce a creamy, slightly sticky rice which is perfect for things like milk puddings, risottos or sushi. Long grain rice stays separate and should be washed well before cooking and not stirred whilst being cooked.

COOKING RICE

There are two very good methods of boiling long grain rice. I normally go for the straightforward Open Pan Method but the Absorption technique is just as successful.

Open Pan Method

Bring a large pan of lightly salted water to the boil. Tip in the rice, stir once and simmer fairly rapidly, uncovered, until the rice is tender. Drain in a sieve and turn out onto a large plate for 2 minutes to allow the grains to dry and separate.

Absorption Method

After weighing the rice tip it into a measuring jug or a mug and take note of the volume before transferring to a saucepan. Now measure twice that volume in cold water and add to the pan with a teaspoon of salt. Bring to the boil, lower the heat to a slow simmer, cover tightly and cook for 15–20 minutes for long grain rice, 10 minutes for basmati and 35–45 minutes for brown.

RICE TYPES

Risotto rice

Risotto rice is a plump, longish, round grain that absorbs lots of liquid and cooks easily without becoming mushy. If stirred frequently during cooking, it gives a very creamy texture. The best risotto rice is Arborio. It is a bit expensive, and in my experience all the risotto rices are good.

Long grain white rice

This is a polished rice that, like most other white rices including risotto and basmati, has had its husk and bran removed. It can be boiled using either of the two methods above or used for biryani or other oven-baked savoury rices where separate grains are preferred.

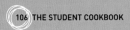

Basmati rice

This is a very delicate, long, slim, fragrant grain that is used extensively in Indian cookery. It is relatively expensive and can be replaced by the usual long grain rice if preferred. It should be washed very well several times and soaked in warm water for 20 minutes before cooking. After soaking it must be handled carefully as the grains are fragile and can easily break. Cook by either of the methods described for just 10 minutes, or use for aromatic pilaf or spiced rice dishes.

Brown rice

Brown rice is a long grain rice which has only had the very tough husk removed, and the bran left intact. It has a nutty flavour and quite a chewy texture, but because of the tough layer it takes about 35–45 minutes to cook and absorbs a lot more water than white. It is, however, not only one of the most flavoursome rices but also the most nutritious. There are lots of other grains and cereals that are used for cooking worldwide. Experiment with different grains, both whole and milled; see Vegetable Couscous (page 137) and Cornbread Chilli Pie (page 136) for more ideas.

SOUPY VEGETABLE RICE

1 tablespoon olive oil

1 onion, finely chopped

2 garlic cloves, finely chopped

1 carrot, finely diced

1 potato, finely diced

60g (2 oz) long grain rice

600 ml (1 pint) vegetable stock

2 tomatoes, skinned and finely chopped

60g (2 oz) frozen peas

1 tablespoon tomato ketchup

2 tablespoons chopped fresh parsley

seasoning

If you want to keep half of this economical dish in the fridge to eat the following day, you may need to add a little extra stock as the rice will absorb a lot of the liquid when it's left to stand.

Heat the oil in a large saucepan and cook the onion, garlic, carrot and potato for 5 minutes until beginning to turn golden brown. Stir in the rice and cook for 1 minute.

Add the stock, bring to the boil and simmer for 10 minutes. Add the tomatoes and peas and simmer for a further 5–10 minutes until the rice and vegetables are tender.

Stir in the ketchup and parsley and season to taste. Divide into bowls and serve.

 REALLY EASY!
 25 MINUTES
 SERVES 2
 V

EGG AND LEMON SOUP

This is a classic Greek rice soup. Unlike the Chinese-style egg soups, the idea is not to have strands of egg, but to cook them gently so they thicken the soup without scrambling.

Place the stock in a large saucepan and bring to the boil. Add the rice, cover and cook for 15–20 minutes until the rice is tender.

Whisk the eggs until frothy, then mix in the lemon juice and a ladle of the hot stock.

Turn the heat down to low, and slowly pour in the egg mixture, stirring constantly until slightly thickened. Take care not to boil the soup or the eggs will curdle.

Season to taste and stir in the parsley.
Serve immediately.

600 ml (1 pint) vegetable stock

60g (2 oz) long grain rice

2 eggs

juice of a lemon

seasoning

1 tablespoon chopped fresh parsley

EASY! 35 MINUTES SERVES 2

RISI E BISI

knob of butter

1 small onion, chopped

2 garlic cloves,
finely chopped

3 rashers streaky bacon,
chopped

125g (4 oz) risotto rice

750 ml (1¼ pints) chicken
or vegetable stock

250g (8 oz) frozen peas

1 tablespoon chopped
fresh parsley

1 tablespoon freshly
grated Parmesan cheese

salt and freshly ground
black pepper

Risi e Bisi is a thick, soupy rice dish that is a speciality of Venice – it simply means rice and peas. Vegetarians can leave out the bacon.

Heat the butter in a large saucepan and gently cook the onion, garlic and bacon for 5 minutes until softened.

Add the rice and cook for a minute. Pour over the stock, stir well and bring to the boil. Cover and simmer, stirring occasionally, for 15 minutes. If it becomes too dry, add a little more stock.

Stir in the peas and cook for 4 minutes. Stir in the parsley, Parmesan and season well to taste. Divide into soup bowls and serve with warm crusty bread.

 REALLY EASY!

 25 MINUTES

 SERVES 2

KEDGEREE

Kedgeree is traditionally served for breakfast, and is guaranteed to get you back on your feet after a night out on the tiles. If you can't face it first thing in the morning, it makes a great supper dish.

Rinse the rice well with cold water. Place in a large saucepan and pour in enough cold water to rise about 2 cm (1 inch) higher than the rice. Stir once only, bring to the boil and simmer for about 15–20 minutes, until the rice is cooked. Drain well in a sieve and set aside for a few minutes for the grains to separate.

Melt the butter in a large frying pan. Add the rice, flaked fish, eggs, parsley, cream if using, and season to taste.

To hard boil an egg – Plunge the egg into a pan of boiling water. Boil steadily over a medium heat for 6 minutes. Run under cold water until the egg is completely cold to prevent the yolk turning grey.

250g (8 oz) long grain rice

30g (1 oz) butter or margarine

2 smoked, peppered mackerel fillets, flaked

2 hard boiled eggs, shelled and roughly chopped

1 tablespoon roughly chopped parsley

4 tablespoons single (pouring) cream (optional)

seasoning

REALLY EASY!

20 MINUTES

SERVES 2

PAELLA

1 tablespoon vegetable oil

1 small onion, chopped

1 garlic clove, chopped

2 chicken drumsticks

600 ml (1 pint) vegetable or chicken stock

180g (6 oz) short grain or risotto rice

2 tomatoes, roughly chopped

250g (8 oz) fresh seafood eg prawns, cod, mussels, squid, all cut into bite-sized pieces or 125g (4 oz) ready prepared seafood cocktail

60g (2 oz) frozen peas

1 tablespoon chopped fresh parsley

seasoning

Creamy rice with chicken and seafood, this dish, made in larger quantities, is great for a party.

Heat the oil in a large pan and fry the onion, garlic and chicken for about 5 minutes. Add the stock, cover and simmer for 15 minutes.

Add the rice and tomatoes and cook, covered, for 20 minutes, stirring regularly. If using raw fish add to the pan after 10 minutes cooking time; if using seafood cocktail add after 15 minutes.

When the rice and chicken are cooked, stir in the peas and parsley and cook for a further 2 minutes. Season to taste and serve.

EASY! **50** MINUTES SERVES **2**

VEGETABLE PAELLA

Paella always contains saffron, which is incredibly expensive. This vegetarian version uses turmeric which adds a wonderful colour and its own flavour to the dish. Of course it is not same as using the real thing but it's a very good substitute.

Heat the oil in a large pan and fry the onion and garlic for 5 minutes until softened. Add the carrot, pepper (capsicum), aubergine (eggplant) and turmeric and cook gently for a further 5 minutes.

Add the rice and cook for 1 minute. Stir in the stock, thyme and seasoning and bring to the boil. Cover and simmer gently, without stirring, for 10 minutes.

Gently stir in the tomatoes and peas and cook for a further 10 minutes until the rice and vegetables are tender. Spoon onto plates and serve.

- 2 tablespoons olive oil
- 1 small onion, chopped
- 1 garlic clove, finely chopped
- 1 large carrot, diced
- 1 red pepper (capsicum), deseeded and diced
- 1 small aubergine (eggplant), diced
- 1 teaspoon turmeric
- 250g (8 oz) long grain rice
- 600 ml (1 pint) vegetable stock
- 1/2 teaspoon dried thyme
- seasoning
- 2 tomatoes, skinned and roughly chopped
- 60g (2 oz) frozen peas

 REALLY EASY!
 35 MINUTES
 SERVES 2
 V

NASI GORENG

180g (6 oz) long grain rice

2 tablespoons vegetable oil

6 spring onions, sliced

1 garlic clove, finely chopped

250g (8 oz) lean beef or pork, cut into thin strips

1 teaspoon chilli powder

2 tablespoons soy sauce

small knob of butter or 1 tablespoon vegetable oil

2 eggs, beaten

seasoning

Nasi Goreng is Indonesian in origin. Serve it with prawn crackers.

Wash the rice well and cook in boiling water for 15–20 minutes until tender. Drain well.

Meanwhile, **heat** the oil in large frying pan and cook the spring onion, garlic and meat for 8 minutes until the vegetables have softened and the meat is cooked through. Stir in the cooked rice, chilli powder and soy sauce. Stir-fry for 5 minutes until piping hot and turn into serving bowls.

Melt the butter in the same frying pan and pour in the beaten egg. Cook for a minute or two on each side and turn out onto a chopping board. Roll up the omelette and cut into slices. Arrange the slices on top of the rice and serve.

EASY!

30 MINUTES

SERVES 2

LAMB BIRYANI

Biryani is traditionally a lamb dish but it needn't be – try a vegetable or chicken version of your own.

Heat the oil in a saucepan and fry the onion, garlic and lamb for 5 minutes until lightly browned. Stir in the curry paste and yogurt, season to taste, cover with a lid and simmer gently for 30 minutes.

Meanwhile, **boil** 600ml (1 pint) of water in a large saucepan. Wash the rice well and add to the pan with the turmeric and a teaspoon of salt. Cook without stirring for 15–20 minutes until the rice is just tender.

Preheat the oven to 180°C, 350°F, Gas 4. Generously butter a casserole dish and spoon in half the rice. Arrange the lamb curry on top and finish with a layer of the remaining rice. Cover with foil and bake for 30 minutes.

1 tablespoon vegetable oil

1 onion, chopped

1 garlic clove, finely chopped

500g (1 lb) lean lamb, diced

2 tablespoons mild curry paste

150 ml (¼ pint) natural yogurt

180g (6 oz) long grain rice

1 teaspoon ground turmeric

seasoning

REALLY EASY!

1 HOUR

SERVES **2**

LEMON CHICKEN RICE

250g (8 oz) long grain rice

juice and grated rind of a lemon

1 tablespoon chopped fresh parsley

1 garlic clove, finely chopped

seasoning

small knob of butter

2 chicken pieces, skinned

600ml (1 pint) chicken stock

Very easy dish of chicken pieces cooked on a bed of lemon-flavoured rice.

Preheat the oven to 180°C, 350°F, Gas 4. Place the rice, lemon rind, parsley, garlic and a little seasoning in a large bowl and mix well together. Tip into a large roasting tin.

Spread the butter over the chicken pieces, sprinkle lightly with salt and pepper and press firmly into the bed of rice.

Mix together the lemon juice and stock and pour over the rice and chicken. Cover with foil and bake for 1 hour, until the chicken is cooked through and the rice is tender.

 REALLY EASY!

 70 MINUTES

 SERVES 2

JAMBALAYA

Jambalaya has no rules. Try adding different vegetables, pieces of cooked chicken or bacon for an equally tasty result. For a vegetarian version replace the salami with 2 sticks thickly sliced celery and 60g (2 oz) tiny button mushrooms.

Heat the oil in a large pan and gently cook the garlic, onion, chilli and pepper (capsicum) for 5 minutes, until softened.

Add the salami, rice, tomatoes and stock, bring to the boil, cover and simmer for 15–20 minutes until the rice is tender and the liquid has been absorbed.

Stir in the parsley and season to taste. Serve the dish immediately.

REALLY EASY!

35 MINUTES

SERVES 2

1 tablespoon vegetable oil

1 garlic clove

1 onion, chopped

1 small hot chilli, chopped

1 red pepper (capsicum), diced

2 Pepperami salami sausages, cut into 1cm ($^1/_2$ inch) thick slices

150g (5 oz) long grain white rice

2 large tomatoes, diced

300 ml ($^1/_2$ pint) vegetable or chicken stock

2 tablespoons chopped fresh parsley

seasoning

CAJUN GUMBO

1 tablespoon vegetable oil

2 rashers streaky bacon

1 chicken breast, cut into small pieces

1 small onion, sliced

250g (8 oz) fresh okra, sliced in half lengthways

400g (14 oz) can chopped tomatoes

150ml (¼ pint) chicken stock

seasoning

125g (4 oz) long grain white rice

125g (4 oz) prawns

1–2 tablespoons chopped fresh coriander

few drops of Tabasco sauce or other Hot Chilli Sauce (page 251)

Like Jambalaya, there is no one way to make a gumbo; as long as it's fairly fiery and contains prawns and okra (also known as ladies fingers), it qualifies.

Heat the oil in a large saucepan and gently fry together the bacon, chicken and onion for 5 minutes. Add the okra and stir-fry for a further 3 minutes.

Add the can of tomatoes and the stock and bring to the boil. Season to taste and simmer, covered, for 15 minutes until the okra is tender and the chicken cooked through.

Meanwhile **cook** the rice using your preferred method as described in the introduction on page 105.

Stir the prawns, coriander and a few shakes of Tabasco into the gumbo and simmer gently for 3 minutes. Spoon the rice into two serving bowls and top with gumbo. Serve hot.

 EASY!

 30 MINUTES

 SERVES 2

HOT TOMATO RISOTTO

A creamy risotto with tomatoes, garlic and chillies.

Heat the oil in a large pan and gently fry the onion, garlic and chillies for 5 minutes until softened. Stir in the rice and cook together for a further 1 minute.

Tip in the can of tomatoes and stir until the juices are absorbed by the rice. Gradually add the stock a little at a time, waiting for the liquid to be absorbed before adding any more, until the rice is cooked. Cook the rice over a fairly high heat stirring frequently. It should take around 20 minutes to absorb the liquid.

When the rice is cooked, stir in the fresh chopped tomatoes, butter, Parmesan and parsley and season to taste. Serve immediately.

REALLY EASY! 30 MINUTES SERVES 2 V

1 tablespoon olive oil

1 small onion, finely chopped

1 garlic clove, crushed

2 hot red chillies, seeded and finely chopped

250g (8 oz) risotto rice

400g (14 oz) can of chopped tomatoes and their juice

900 ml (1$\frac{1}{2}$ pints) vegetable stock

4 tomatoes, skinned and roughly chopped

30g (1 oz) butter

2 tablespoons freshly grated Parmesan cheese

2 tablespoons chopped fresh parsley

seasoning

CHINESE EGG-FRIED RICE

180g (6 oz) long grain rice

2 tablespoons vegetable oil

2 eggs, beaten

1 chicken breast, shredded

1 cm (¹/₂ inch) piece fresh ginger, grated

1 carrot, cut into matchsticks

bunch of spring onions, thickly sliced on the diagonal

125g (4 oz) can sliced water chestnuts

60g (2 oz) prawns

1 tablespoon soy sauce

The secret of egg-fried rice is to cook the egg separately. If you add raw egg to the hot rice whilst in the pan, it will simply absorb the egg and become sticky.

Wash the rice well and cook in boiling water for 15–20 minutes until tender. Drain well.

Heat a little of the oil in a wok or large frying pan. Tip in the beaten eggs and using a chop stick, stir until set. Remove from the wok and set aside.

Heat the remaining vegetable oil in the wok and quickly stir-fry the chicken, ginger, and carrot sticks for 5 minutes over a high heat until the chicken is cooked through.

Stir in the spring onions, water chestnuts, prawns, cooked rice and egg, mixing well together. Add soy sauce, continue stir-frying until heated right through and serve.

EASY!

35 MINUTES

SERVES **2**

CARIBBEAN RICE

An exotic flavoured rice dish with ginger, chilli, pineapple, coconut and almonds.

Heat the oil in a large saucepan and cook the onion, ginger and chilli for 10 minutes until softened and golden brown. Add the rice and cook for 1 minute.

Stir in the pineapple chunks with the juice, the vegetable stock, coconut, if using, and seasoning. Bring to the boil, stir once, cover and simmer gently for 20 minutes until the grains are tender.

Gently stir in the parsley and almonds and serve immediately.

 REALLY EASY!
 35 MINUTES
 SERVES 2
 V

1 tablespoon vegetable oil

1 large onion, sliced

1 teaspoon finely grated root ginger

1 small red chilli, seeded and finely chopped

250g (8 oz) long grain rice

200g (7 oz) can pineapple chunks in natural juice

450 ml ($^3/_4$ pint) vegetable stock

1 tablespoon dessicated coconut (optional)

seasoning

1 tablespoon chopped fresh parsley

1 tablespoon toasted flaked almonds

BAKED TOMATO RICE CAKE

Give a new lease of life to leftover risotto by turning it into a baked rice cake. Use any type of risotto, such as the mushroom risotto on page 125 or like the one below, tomato. Cut the cake into wedges and serve with salad.

Heat the oil in a large pan and gently fry the onion and garlic for 5 minutes until softened. Stir in the rice and sun dried tomatoes and cook together for 1 minute.

Tip in the can of tomatoes and stir until the juices are absorbed by the rice. Gradually add the stock a little at a time, waiting for the liquid to be absorbed before adding any more, until the rice is cooked. Keep the rice over a fairly high heat, stir it frequently and it should take about 20 minutes.

When the rice is cooked, stir in the butter, Parmesan and parsley and season to taste. Leave the risotto to cool for 5 minutes.

Preheat the oven to 180°C, 350°F, Gas 4. Turn the mixture into a deep cake tin. Beat together the eggs and milk, season lightly and pour over the mixture. Sprinkle on the mozzarella and use a chopstick or a fork to loosely blend the mixture together. Bake for 25 minutes until set.

1 tablespoon olive oil

1 small onion, finely chopped

1 garlic clove, crushed

250g (8 oz) risotto rice

8 sun dried tomatoes in oil, finely shredded

400g (14 oz) can of chopped tomatoes

900 ml (1 1/2 pints) vegetable stock

30g (1 oz) butter

2 tablespoons freshly grated Parmesan cheese

2 tablespoons chopped fresh parsley

seasoning

2 eggs

150 ml (1/4 pint) milk

125g (4 oz) mozzarella cheese, diced

EASY!

1 HOUR

SERVES 2

BROCCOLI AND ALMOND PILAF

1 tablespoon olive oil

1 small onion, chopped

1 teaspoon curry paste

250g (8 oz) easy-cook brown rice

450 ml (^{3}/4 pint) vegetable stock

250g (8 oz) broccoli, broken into florets

250g (8 oz) button mushrooms, halved

seasoning

30g (1 oz) toasted flaked almonds

A brown rice pilaf with a hint of curry, containing broccoli, onion, mushrooms and topped with toasted flaked almonds.

Heat the oil in a large frying pan. Stir-fry the onion and curry paste for 5 minutes. Add the rice and stir for a further minute.

Pour in the stock and bring to the boil. Stir once, then cover and simmer for 30 minutes. Add the broccoli and mushrooms, cover and simmer for a further 10 minutes. Season to taste and serve sprinkled with flaked almonds.

 REALLY EASY!

 45 MINUTES

 SERVES 2

 V

MUSHROOM RISOTTO

A good risotto should be creamy with soft but not mushy grains. It might take a couple of attempts to get right, but once you have it perfected, there is no end to the variations you can develop yourself. Try using canned or sun dried tomatoes, different herbs or green vegetables. If you feel like treating yourself, substitute a glass of wine (white or red) for some of the stock.

Heat the oil in a large pan and gently fry the onion and garlic for 5 minutes until softened. Stir in the rice and mushrooms and cook together for 1 minute.

Gradually **add** the stock a little at a time, waiting for the liquid to be absorbed before adding any more, until all the liquid is absorbed and the rice is cooked. Keep the rice over a fairly high heat, stir it frequently and it should take 20 minutes. If it takes longer than this, the rice will become too soft, so don't be afraid to raise the heat.

When the rice is cooked, stir in the butter, Parmesan and parsley. Season to taste and serve immediately.

1 tablespoon olive oil

1 small onion, finely chopped

1 garlic clove, crushed

250g (8 oz) risotto rice

250g (8 oz) flat mushrooms, sliced

900 ml (1$\frac{1}{2}$ pints) vegetable stock

30g (1 oz) butter

2 tablespoons freshly grated Parmesan cheese

2 tablespoons chopped fresh parsley

seasoning

REALLY EASY!

30 MINUTES

SERVES **2**

V

MUSHROOM AND EGG PILAF

2 tablespoons vegetable oil

1 small onion, chopped

1 teaspoon hot curry paste

250g (8 oz) mushrooms, thickly sliced

250g (8 oz) long grain rice

450 ml ($^3/_4$ pint) vegetable stock

1 tablespoon mango chutney

2 eggs, beaten

1 garlic clove, finely chopped

1 tablespoon finely chopped coriander

seasoning

Rice with onion and mushrooms, flavoured with curry and mango chutney with sliced omelette stirred in at the end.

Heat a tablespoon of the oil in a large saucepan with a close-fitting lid. Cook the onion and curry paste for 5 minutes until softened. Add the mushrooms and rice and cook for a further 1 minute.

Pour in the stock and chutney and bring to the boil. Stir once, then cover and simmer very gently for 20 minutes.

Meanwhile, **beat** together the eggs, garlic, coriander and a little seasoning. Heat a little of the remaining oil in a small frying pan and pour in the eggs. Cook gently until golden brown underneath and almost set. Flip over and cook the second side.

Cut the thick omelette into bite-size pieces and when the rice is tender, fork into the pilaf. Season to taste and serve.

 EASY!
 30 MINUTES
 SERVES 2
 V

ORANGE RICE

For extra flavour, toast the peanuts for a few minutes under a hot grill, stirring occasionally until golden.

Heat the oil in a large saucepan and cook the onion and carrot for 5 minutes until they begin to turn golden brown. Add the rice and cook for a further 1 minute.

Add the orange juice and vegetable stock. Cover and simmer for 10 minutes.

Stir in the peas and sweetcorn and continue to cook for a further 5 minutes until the rice and vegetables are tender.

Add the peanuts, parsley and orange rind. Check the seasoning and serve.

REALLY EASY! · 25 MINUTES · SERVES 2 · V

2 tablespoons vegetable oil

1 small onion, finely chopped

1 carrot, cut into small dice

250g (8 oz) long grain rice

juice and finely grated rind of 2 large oranges

450 ml ($^{3}/_{4}$ pint) vegetable stock

60g (2 oz) frozen peas

60g (2 oz) frozen sweetcorn

60g (2 oz) salted peanuts

1 tablespoon chopped fresh parsley

seasoning

RICE AND LENTILS

2 tablespoons vegetable oil

1 large onion, chopped

2 garlic cloves, finely chopped

2 celery sticks, chopped

1 small red chilli, seeded and finely chopped

250g (8 oz) long grain rice

180g (6 oz) red lentils

2 tomatoes, skinned and chopped

900 ml (1¹/₂ pints) vegetable stock

seasoning

This is a brilliant emergency dish that you can make almost entirely with store cupboard ingredients. If you're really broke, you can make it with just onions, rice and lentils.

Heat the oil in a large pan and cook the onion, garlic, celery and chilli for 5 minutes until softened. Add the rice and cook for a further 1 minute.

Stir in the lentils, tomatoes and stock. Bring to the boil, cover and simmer for 15–20 minutes until the rice and lentils are tender. Do not stir the rice but check it to make sure it hasn't boiled dry, adding more stock or water if necessary.

Season to taste, spoon onto plates and serve.

 REALLY EASY!

 25 MINUTES

 SERVES 2

 V

CARROT AND COURGETTE RICE PATTIES

This a great way to use up leftover rice. The patties are quite crumbly when being shaped but once in the pan, they cook beautifully with a crunchy coating and soft, melting centre.

Stir together the rice, courgette (zucchini), carrot, cheese, garlic, parsley, 1 tablespoon of flour, 1 beaten egg and plenty of seasoning.

Shape into 6 round, flat patties. Coat in flour, then in egg and finally breadcrumbs.

Heat 2.5 cm (1 inch) of oil in a small deep frying pan and cook the patties for 3–4 minutes on each side, until golden brown. Drain on kitchen paper and serve with tomato ketchup or Hot Chilli Sauce (page 251) and salad.

EASY!

35 MINUTES

SERVES 2

180g (6 oz) cooked long grain rice

1 courgette (zucchini), finely grated

1 carrot, finely grated

60g (2 oz) finely grated Gruyère or Cheddar cheese

1 garlic clove, crushed

1 tablespoon chopped fresh parsley

3 tablespoons plain flour

2 eggs

seasoning

6 tablespoons fresh breadcrumbs

vegetable oil, for frying

RASTAFARIAN RICE AND BEANS

250g (8 oz) brown rice

150 ml (1¼ pint) coconut milk

1½ teaspoon dried thyme

400g (14 oz) can black-eye beans, drained

seasoning

Rice and Beans is a traditional Rastafarian dish, though to really eat rasta, to be 'irie' (at one with nature), you should shun any additives, or processed foods, which means no canned beans and no salt!

Wash the rice well and place in a large saucepan with the coconut milk, thyme and 300 ml (½ pint) water. Bring to the boil, cover and simmer gently for 15 minutes.

Add the beans, season to taste and cook together for a further 10 minutes until the rice is tender.

 REALLY EASY!
 30 MINUTES
 SERVES 2
 V

APPLEY RICE SALAD

A fresh tasting rice salad with apples, cheese, onion and red peppers (capsicum).

Wash the rice well and cook in boiling water for 15–20 minutes until tender. Drain well and set aside to go cold.

Meanwhile, **dice** and core the apples and toss in the lime juice. Place in a large bowl with the red onion, cheese, red pepper (capsicum), olive oil, rice, herbs and seasoning. Toss well together and serve.

 REALLY EASY!
 20 MINUTES
 SERVES 2
 V

180g (6 oz) long grain rice

2 green apples

juice and grated rind of a lime

1 red onion, finely chopped

125g (4 oz) cheese, eg Cheddar, Edam, diced

1 red pepper (capsicum), diced

2 tablespoons olive oil

1 tablespoon chopped fresh coriander or parsley

seasoning

TABBOULEH

125g (4 oz) bulgar wheat

2 tomatoes, chopped

4 spring onions, sliced

125g (4 oz) feta cheese, crumbled or diced

2–3 tablespoons finely chopped parsley

juice of a lemon

3 tablespoons olive oil

seasoning

This classic Lebanese salad is based on bulgar wheat, also labelled as cracked wheat. When you buy it in the shops, it has already been cooked and then dried so it just needs rehydrating with a little boiling water. Keep it cool and dry in your cupboard and it will last for months. The addition of Greek feta cheese makes tabbouleh taste even better. Eat with warm pitta bread or use it to stuff hollowed-out beef tomatoes.

Put the bulgar wheat in a large bowl and fill with boiling water. Set aside for 20 minutes until the grains have swollen and absorbed most of the water. Drain very well and return to the bowl.

Stir in the tomatoes, spring onion, feta, parsley, lemon juice and olive oil. Mix well together, season to taste and serve.

REALLY EASY! · 20 MINUTES · SERVES 2 · V

WARM BULGAR WHEAT SALAD

Add variety to this simple supper dish by serving the grilled vegetables on a bed of rice or couscous in place of the bulgar wheat.

Place the stock in a saucepan and bring to the boil. Tip in the bulgar wheat, turn off the heat and cover with a lid. Leave the grains for 20 minutes to absorb the water and puff up while you grill the vegetables.

Arrange the vegetables in the grill pan and brush with the tablespoon of olive oil. Sprinkle lightly with salt and grill for about 8 minutes on each side until tender and golden.

Meanwhile **make** the dressing by whisking all the ingredients together with a fork. Spoon the warm bulgar wheat onto two plates and arrange the grilled vegetables on top. Drizzle over the dressing and serve immediately.

REALLY EASY!   30 MINUTES   SERVES 2   V

300 ml (1 1/2 pint) vegetable stock

125g (4 oz) bulgar wheat

1 courgette (zucchini), sliced lengthways

1 small aubergine (eggplant), sliced lengthways

1 red pepper (capsicum), cut into 8 strips, lengthways

125g (4 oz) large mushrooms, thickly sliced

1 tablespoon olive oil

For The Dressing

2 tablespoons olive oil

juice of half a lemon

1 garlic clove, finely chopped

1 tablespoon chopped fresh parsley

pinch of sugar

seasoning

PESTO AUBERGINES WITH BULGAR WHEAT

125g (4 oz) bulgar wheat

1 large aubergine (eggplant)

1 tablespoon olive oil

2 tomatoes, skinned and finely diced

1 tablespoon freshly grated Parmesan cheese

For the Dressing

2 tablespoons purchased pesto sauce

2 tablespoons olive oil

juice of half a lemon

salt and freshly ground black pepper

Serve the aubergines (eggplant) on your choice of cooked grain – couscous also works very well.

Put the bulgar wheat in a large bowl and fill with boiling water. Set aside for 20 minutes until the grains have swollen and absorbed most of the water. Drain.

Slice the aubergines (eggplant) lengthwise into 1 cm (¹/₂ inch) thick slices. Brush with oil and place under a preheated grill for 6–10 minutes until golden and tender.

Spoon the warm bulgar wheat onto plates and arrange the aubergine (eggplant) slices on top. Sprinkle over the tomatoes and scatter with the Parmesan.

Whisk together the pesto, olive oil, lemon juice, a little salt and plenty of black pepper. Drizzle the dressing over the aubergines (eggplant) and serve while still warm.

 REALLY EASY!

 25 MINUTES

 SERVES 2

 ✓

BULGAR WHEAT SALAD

Eat this crunchy salad with pitta bread for a light lunch or supper or if you're really hungry, serve as an accompaniment to Seedy Bean Burgers (page 218) or Stuffed Mushrooms (page 214).

Put the bulgar wheat in a large bowl and fill with boiling water. Set aside for 20 minutes until the grains have swollen and absorbed most of the water. Drain well and return to the bowl.

Stir in the pepper (capsicum), carrot, garlic, onion, peanuts and raisins, mixing well together. Spoon onto serving plates.

Whisk together the soft cheese, lemon juice, olive oil and seasoning and drizzle over the salad.

125g (4 oz) bulgar wheat

1 green pepper (capsicum), deseeded and cut into small dice

1 large carrot, cut into small dice

1 garlic clove, finely chopped

1 onion, finely chopped

125g (4 oz) packet of peanuts and raisins

60g (2 oz) soft cheese

juice of a lemon

3 tablespoons olive oil

seasoning

 REALLY EASY! 25 MINUTES SERVES 2 √

CORNBREAD CHILLI PIE

1 tablespoon sunflower or vegetable oil

1 onion, chopped

2 garlic cloves, finely chopped

2 hot chillies, finely chopped

1 green pepper (capsicum), diced

400g (14 oz) can red kidney beans, drained

400g (14 oz) can chopped tomatoes

few drops of Tabasco sauce or other hot chilli sauce

seasoning

For The Cornbread

125g (4 oz) fine cornmeal

1 tablespoon plain flour

$^{1}/_{2}$ teaspoon salt

2 teaspoons baking powder

1 egg, beaten

6 tablespoons milk

1 tablespoon sunflower or vegetable oil

Cornmeal is the basis of many dishes, from the Northern Italian speciality 'polenta' to this favourite of southern USA.

Preheat the oven to 220°C, 425°F, Gas 7. Heat the oil and fry the onion, garlic, chillies and pepper (capsicum) for about 5 minutes until softened. Add the kidney beans, tomatoes, Tabasco and season to taste. Bring to the boil and simmer for 10 minutes.

Place the cornmeal, flour, salt and baking powder in a bowl and make a well in the centre. Add the egg, milk and vegetable oil and mix well together with a wooden spoon.

Transfer the chilli mixture to a deep baking dish and spoon on top the cornbread mixture. Smooth the top with the back of a spoon and bake for 25 minutes until firm.

 EASY! 45 MINUTES SERVES 2 V

VEGETABLE COUSCOUS

Couscous is a typical Middle Eastern ingredient. Although often used in the same way as other grains, it is actually derived from the root of the cassava plant, and is related to semolina.

Put the couscous in a bowl and cover with boiling water for 10 minutes until it has swollen.

Meanwhile, **heat** the oil in a saucepan and cook the onion, garlic, aubergine (eggplant), carrot and cumin for 5 minutes. Stir in the tomatoes, purée, vegetable stock and chick-peas and bring to the boil.

Line a metal sieve with a very clean tea towel and place over the pan. Tip in the couscous. Cover the pan with foil, to enclose the steam and simmer very gently for 25 minutes until the vegetables are tender.

Fluff up the couscous with a fork and divide onto plates. Stir the chopped coriander and peanuts into the vegetables and season to taste. Spoon onto the bed of couscous and serve.

180g (6 oz) couscous

2 tablespoons vegetable oil

1 onion, roughly chopped

1 garlic clove, finely chopped

1 small aubergine (eggplant), diced

1 carrot, sliced

1/2 teaspoon ground cumin

2 tomatoes, chopped

1 tablespoon tomato purée

300 ml (1/2 pint) vegetable stock

200g (7 oz) can chick-peas, drained

1 tablespoon chopped fresh coriander

60g (2 oz) peanuts

seasoning

REALLY EASY!

35 MINUTES

SERVES **2**

V

CHICK-PEA AND TOMATO COUSCOUS

180g (6 oz) couscous

2 tablespoons vegetable oil

1 onion, roughly chopped

1 garlic clove, finely chopped

1 cm ($\frac{1}{2}$ inch) piece fresh root ginger, peeled and finely chopped

$\frac{1}{2}$ teaspoon ground cumin

4 tomatoes, skinned and roughly chopped

150 ml ($\frac{1}{4}$ pint) vegetable stock

400g (14 oz) can chick-peas, drained

4 tablespoons Greek yogurt

1 tablespoon chopped fresh coriander

60g (2 oz) cashew nuts (optional)

seasoning

If you're feeling flush, add the cashew nuts to this dish, if not, use peanuts or leave them out altogether.

Put the couscous in a bowl and cover with boiling water for 10 minutes until it has swollen.

Meanwhile, **heat** the oil in a saucepan and cook the onion, garlic, ginger and cumin for 5 minutes until softened. Stir in the tomatoes, vegetable stock and chick-peas and bring to the boil.

Line a metal sieve with a new paper kitchen cloth or a very clean tea towel and place over the pan. Tip in the couscous. Cover the pan with foil, to enclose the steam and simmer very gently for 15 minutes until the stew is thickened and the couscous is piping hot.

Fluff up the couscous with a fork and divide onto plates. Stir the yogurt, chopped coriander and nuts if using, into the stew and season to taste. Spoon onto the bed of couscous and serve.

 EASY! **30** MINUTES

 SERVES **2** V

JANE'S PEANUT NOODLES

Vegetarian student Jane, who was my flatmate, managed to include peanut butter in just about every dish she cooks. In this recipe it tastes delicious.

Cook the noodles according to packet instructions, drain and set aside.

Meanwhile, **heat** the oil in a wok or large frying pan and stir-fry the onion, garlic, chilli, carrot and mushrooms for 5 minutes until beginning to brown.

Add the peanut butter, creamed coconut, soy sauce and 2 tablespoons of water, and cook for a further 2–3 minutes until the vegetables are tender.

Stir in the spinach and noodles and season to taste. Heat through for 1–2 minutes until piping hot and serve immediately.

125g (4 oz) Chinese egg noodles

1 tablespoon vegetable oil

1 onion, roughly chopped

1 garlic clove, thinly sliced

1 hot red chilli, seeded and finely chopped

1 carrot, sliced

125g (4 oz) button mushrooms, halved

3 tablespoons crunchy peanut butter

60g (2 oz) creamed coconut

1 tablespoon soy sauce

125g (4 oz) frozen leaf spinach, thawed

seasoning

 REALLY EASY!
 10 MINUTES
 SERVES 2
 V

BREAD AND FLOUR

There's nothing in the world more appetising than the smell of freshly baking bread. When you walk into a supermarket that has an in-store bakery, you will always catch the smell of the bread. I'm not sure if they plan it purposefully as the bakery always seems to be at the other side of the shop, but it certainly sets your tummy rumbling and your hand reaching out for a currant bun.

INTRODUCTION

The range of breads now readily available is quite incredible. It is easy to buy freshly baked bread in all shapes, sizes, textures and flavours, from Italian olive breads to Greek pittas and Irish soda bread. With such a choice, there's no reason why bread shouldn't be a fundamental part of your diet.

STORING BREAD

If you buy your bread fresh from a bakery, it is best eaten the day you buy it but it will last a couple of days if you store it in a cool, dry cupboard in its paper wrapper to allow the bread to breathe. If it goes hard the next day, pop into a hot oven for 5 minutes to heat through and soften. If you buy sliced, plastic wrapped bread, you can store it for longer because of the additives used in large scale bread production, but it will go mouldy rather than hard after a few days. If you can't eat a whole loaf within a week, keep it in the freezer and pull out slices as you need them.

FLOUR

Even if you're not a baker, you should always make sure you have a small packet of plain flour in your cupboard. Use it to thicken soups and sauces, coat meat and vegetables for frying as in the courgette (zucchini) wheels (page 237) and barbecued spare ribs (page 230), to roll out ready-made pastry, make dumplings (page 163) and batters for pancakes (page 156) and Toad in the Hole (page 161). If you can remember learning to make puff pastry at school, you will be able to appreciate why ready-made pastry is such a blessing. It can be bought both fresh and frozen and you will only need to use half a packet to make enough for two, and the remainder can be kept covered in the fridge for a couple of days.

EGGY BREAD SANDWICH

Use any filling you like for this sandwich but cheese works particularly well. If you have any egg mixture left over, pour it on top of the bread as it is cooking in the pan.

Mix together the cheese, mayonnaise and onion and spread thickly on a slice of the bread. Top with the other slice to make a sandwich.

Beat the egg, milk and a little seasoning together in a shallow dish and lay in the sandwich. Press down with a spatula so the bread absorbs the liquid. Leave to soak for 15–20 minutes.

Heat a little oil in a frying pan and cook the bread for 3–4 minutes on each side until puffed and golden brown. Drain on kitchen paper and eat straightaway.

60g (2 oz) grated cheese

1 tablespoon mayonnaise

1 spring onion, finely chopped (optional)

2 slices white bread

1 egg

2 tablespoons milk

seasoning

vegetable oil, for frying

REALLY EASY!

30 MINUTES

SERVES 2

TABLE-TOP NAAN

250g (8 oz) self-raising flour

1 teaspoon easy-blend dried yeast

3 tablespoons live natural yogurt

1 teaspoon salt

small knob of butter

Definitely the most fashionable food to be seen eating is a balti curry which has to be served with the compulsory table-top naan. Impress your friends with your own, home-made bumper naan breads. To make sesame and coriander naan, add 1 teaspoon finely chopped fresh coriander to the dry flour mixture. When the dough is rolled out, press 1–2 tablespoons sesame seeds into both sides of each naan. Bake as below.

Place the flour, yeast and salt together in a large bowl and make a well in the centre. Spoon in the yogurt and gradually add about 6 tablespoons of warm water, bringing the mixture together to form a very soft, slightly sticky dough. Knead lightly for 1 minute then cover with a tea towel and leave in a warm place for about an hour.

Preheat the grill to high. Divide the dough into two equal pieces and roll out on a lightly floured surface into two large rectangles, each as big as your grill pan. Place under the grill for about 1 minute on the first side and 30 seconds on the other, until puffed and lightly browned. When the naans are ready, and still hot, spread them with a little butter.

 EASY! 1 HOUR SERVES 2 V

CHEESY KIPPER TOASTS

Boil-in-the-bag kippers are a great invention – it means that you can eat kippers whenever you want without them leaving their odour on your grill pan for weeks. If you like, try this recipe with peppered mackerel fillets.

Cook the kippers according to packet instructions. Mash well with a fork and mix in the cheese, yogurt and Worcestershire sauce.

Spread the mixture onto the toast and sprinkle generously with black pepper. Place under a hot grill for 3–4 minutes until bubbling and golden. Eat straight away.

REALLY EASY!

30 MINUTES

SERVES 2

1 pack boil-in-the-bag kippers

60g (2 oz) Cheddar cheese, grated

3 tablespoons Greek yogurt

1 teaspoon Worcestershire sauce

2 large, thick slices of hot buttered toast

freshly ground black pepper

SAUCY STIR-FRY ON TOAST

1 large potato, peeled and diced

1 tablespoon vegetable oil

2 bacon rashers, roughly chopped (optional)

2 leeks, sliced

1 apple, diced

3 leaves Savoy cabbage, shredded

2 tablespoon soy sauce

2 large, thick slices of hot buttered toast

seasoning

A strange sounding name for a fabulously, warming dish that takes just a few minutes to prepare.

Par-cook the potatoes in boiling, salted water for 5 minutes.

Meanwhile, add the oil to a wok or large frying pan and **stir-fry** the bacon and leeks for 3 minutes. Add the drained potato cubes and continue to cook for 5 minutes. Add the apple, cabbage, soy sauce and about 5 tablespoons of water and cook for a further 5 minutes.

Pile on top of the hot buttered toast and serve immediately.

 REALLY EASY!

 25 MINUTES

 SERVES 1

MEDITERRANEAN OPEN SANDWICH

All supermarkets and most bakeries now stock ciabatta, the chewy Italian bread made with olive oil. Its firm texture makes it a great base for open sandwiches.

Split the loaf in half through the middle. Place the olives and garlic on a board and chop together finely with a heavy knife until blended. Transfer to a small bowl and stir in a tablespoon of the olive oil.

Spread the mixture onto the cut surfaces of the bread and place under a hot grill for 3–4 minutes until crisp and golden.

Place the avocado, tomato, mozzarella, spring onion, remaining olive oil and lemon juice in a bowl. Toss well together and season to taste. Pile on top of the bread and serve immediately.

1 loaf ciabatta bread

60g (2 oz) pitted black olives

1 garlic clove

3 tablespoons olive oil

1 avocado, diced

2 tomatoes, diced

150g (5 oz) mozzarella cheese, diced

6 spring onions, sliced thickly

juice of half a lemon

seasoning

 REALLY EASY!

 10 MINUTES

 SERVES 2

V

HOT TOMATO BAGUETTE

1 French stick

2 tablespoons pesto sauce

4 large tomatoes, sliced

1 tablespoon olive oil

1 garlic clove, finely chopped

1 tablespoon freshly grated Parmesan cheese

seasoning

Try topping these with some grated mozzarella or thin slices of onion or courgette.

Preheat the oven to 200°C, 400°F, Gas 6. Split the French stick in half lengthways. Spread thinly with pesto sauce and arrange the tomato slices on top.

Brush the tomatoes with olive oil and sprinkle with garlic, Parmesan. and seasoning. Bake directly on the oven shelf for about 8 minutes until hot and crunchy.

REALLY EASY!
 10 MINUTES
SERVES 2
 V

FATTOUSH

Fattoush is a Lebanese salad that has pieces of crisply toasted pitta bread tossed in just before serving. It make a great lunch in summer.

Toss together the cucumber, pepper (capsicum), tomatoes and spring onions.

Break the pittas into bite-size pieces and add to the salad.

Whisk together the lemon juice, olive oil and plenty of seasoning. Pour over the salad, toss well together and serve immediately.

REALLY EASY! 5 MINUTES SERVES 2

1 mini cucumber, diced

1 large red pepper (capsicum), diced

2 firm tomatoes, diced

bunch spring onions, thickly sliced

2 tablespoons chopped fresh parsley

3 pitta breads, toasted until crisp and golden

juice of half a lemon

3 tablespoons olive oil

seasoning

BASIC PIZZA DOUGH

400g (14 oz) plain flour

2 teaspoons easy-blend dried yeast

1 teaspoon salt

2 tablespoons olive oil

Place the flour, yeast and salt in a large bowl. Make a well in the centre and pour in 250 ml (8 floz) water. Using your hand to mix, bring the ingredients together to form a soft, pliable dough. Turn the dough out onto a lightly floured work surface and knead vigorously for at least 5 minutes until the dough is smooth and stretchy. Because all flours are slightly different, you may find that you need to add extra flour or water to get a good, soft but not too sticky dough.

Rub a little oil over the surface of the ball of dough, put into a large bowl and cover with a clean tea towel and leave in a warm place for about 30 minutes until doubled in size. Divide the dough into four equal balls and knead them again for a couple of minutes. Roll out the dough to the size and thickness you like, remembering that it will be at least double in thickness by the time it is cooked, and place on baking sheets/trays.

Preheat the oven to 240ºC, 475ºF, Gas 9. Arrange the toppings on your pizzas, except the cheese, if using, and place in the oven for 10 minutes. Sprinkle over the cheese and return to the oven for a further 5–10 minutes until the pizza is crisp and golden brown.

EASY!

1 HOUR

MAKES 4

V

PIZZA TOPPINGS

The quickest and one of the best sauces to use as a base for pizza is passata. This can be bought from most supermarkets in a carton or bottle and is made from sieved plum tomatoes. Spread it over the dough, sprinkle with a little good olive oil and season lightly with salt, pepper and some dried oregano or basil before adding your choice of toppings. The quantities given are for each individual pizza.

V Marinara the original pizza 2–3 tablespoons passata, pinch dried oregano, 1 finely chopped garlic clove, 1 teaspoon olive oil, seasoning.

Neopolitana 2–3 tablespoons passata, 2 canned anchovy fillets, 6 pickled capers, 4 black olives, 1 teaspoon olive oil, 30g (1 oz) chopped mozzarella cheese, seasoning.

Pescatora 2–3 tablespoons passata, pinch dried basil, 60g (2 oz) ready-prepared seafood cocktail, 1 finely chopped garlic clove, 1 teaspoon olive oil, seasoning.

V Funghi 2–3 tablespoons passata, pinch dried oregano, 60g (2 oz) sliced mushrooms, 1 chopped garlic clove, 30g (1 oz) chopped mozzarella cheese, 1 teaspoon olive oil

V Margherita 2–3 tablespoons passata, 60g (2 oz) chopped mozzarella cheese, pinch dried oregano, 1 teaspoon olive oil, seasoning.

V Florentina 2–3 tablespoons passata, 60g (2 oz) frozen chopped or leaf spinach (thawed), 1 egg, 30g (1 oz) chopped mozzarella cheese, seasoning. Use the spinach to make a border around the pizza, crack the egg into the hollow and sprinkle over the cheese and seasoning.

CALAZONE WITH COURGETTES

1 large courgette
(zucchini)

1 large onion,
finely chopped

2 garlic cloves,
finely chopped

2 tablespoons chopped
fresh parsley

4 tablespoons olive oil,
plus extra for brushing

seasoning

$1/2$ quantity pizza dough
(page 150)

flour for rolling

This delicious calazone can be cut into squares and eaten cold for a packed lunch. If you want to reheat it, place the squares under a low grill for about 10 minutes until warmed through and crisp.

Preheat the oven to 240°C, 475°F, Gas 9. Quarter the courgettes (zucchini) lengthways then slice very thinly widthways to make little wedges. Toss with the onion, garlic, parsley, oil and plenty of seasoning.

Divide the dough in half and roll out on a floured surface to make 2 large, thin rectangles about 25 cm x 38 cm (10 inch x 15 inch). Place one half on a lightly-oiled baking sheet/tray and scatter over the filling, leaving a 1cm ($1/2$ inch) border. Dampen the edges and cover with the other rectangle of dough, pressing with your fingers to seal.

Brush the top with a little olive oil and bake in the oven for 15–20 minutes until crisp and golden.

 REALLY EASY!

 25 MINUTES

 SERVES 2

 V

CALAZONE WITH CHEESY POTATOES

The Parmesan is rolled into the dough and gives a delicious flavour to the crust. These giant pizza pies will really fill you up, so be prepared to eat well.

Cook the potatoes in plenty of boiling salted water for 10–15 minutes until tender. Drain well and mash with the milk until smooth and fluffy. Stir in the cheese, onion, basil and plenty of seasoning.

Preheat the oven to 220°C, 450°F, Gas 7. Sprinkle a little flour and the Parmesan onto the work surface. Divide the dough in half and roll out on the work surface into 2 very thin 30 cm (12 inch) rounds. Spoon the cheesy potato onto one side of each of the rounds. Dampen the edges and fold over the dough, pressing with your fingers to seal.

Place the calazone on a lightly-oiled baking sheet/tray and bend the 2 corners towards each other to form a crescent shape. Bake for 15–20 minutes until crusty and golden.

500g (1 lb) old potatoes, diced

2 tablespoons milk

125g (4 oz) mature Cheddar cheese, grated

1 small onion, finely chopped

few leaves fresh basil, roughly torn

seasoning

flour for rolling

2 tablespoons freshly grated Parmesan cheese

1/2 quantity pizza dough (page 150)

 REALLY EASY!
 45 MINUTES
 SERVES 2

FRYING PAN PIZZA

125g (4 oz) self-raising
flour

pinch of salt

2 tablespoons olive oil

If you fancy a pizza just for yourself, but don't have
the time or energy for making up some bread dough,
this delicious frying-pan pizza is quick, simple and
just as tasty.

Place the flour and salt in a bowl. Make a well in the
centre and add 3 tablespoons of water and 1 tablespoon
of olive oil. Mix together to make a firm dough.

Shape the mixture into a ball and then flatten or roll
out to fit a small frying pan. Heat the remaining oil in
the pan and fry the pizza base for about 5 minutes
until golden brown.

Flip over and cook the other side for 5 minutes, slide
onto a plate and serve with a topping of your choice,
eg. a fried egg and halved tomato. Alternatively, cover
the uncooked top with a cheesy mixture (see opposite)
and place under a hot grill for 5 minutes until bubbling
and golden. Eat immediately.

REALLY EASY! — 15 MINUTES — SERVES 1 — ✓

CHEESY TOPPINGS

(V) Cream cheese and chopped fresh herbs

(V) Sliced Cheddar cheese and tomatoes

(V) 2 tablespoons passata sprinkled with grated Cheddar cheese

(V) Grated cheese mixed with butter and mustard

(V) Mushrooms fried in butter and garlic sprinkled with grated cheese

(V) Mozzarella cheese and slivers of sun dried tomato

(V) Small can of baked beans topped with grated Cheddar cheese

PANCAKES
BASIC PANCAKES

125g (4 oz) flour

1/4 teaspoon of salt

1 egg, beaten

300 ml (1/2 pint) milk

small knob of butter, melted

vegetable oil, for frying

Pancakes are a fantastic base for lots of different meals. They are used extensively in Mexican, Chinese and French cooking as well as English. Why wait until Pancake Day, try cooking some of the following recipes next time you're stuck for ideas.

Sieve the flour and salt into a bowl and make a well in the centre.

Add the egg and milk and whisk vigorously to make a smooth batter. Beat in the melted butter.

Heat a little oil in a small, shallow non-stick frying pan. Spoon in 2 tablespoons of mixture and swirl to cover the base of the pan. Cook for a few seconds, flip over and cook the second side. Repeat to make 8 pancakes in total.

EASY! **10** MINUTES MAKES **8**

PANCAKES
SPINACH PANCAKES

This pancake batter has spinach added to it for extra flavour. Try with one of the suggested savoury fillings for a tasty snack or supper dish.

Sieve the flour and salt into a large bowl. Make a well in the centre and add the egg and milk. Beat together until smooth. Squeeze the spinach to remove any excess water, then stir into the batter.

Heat a little oil in a small, shallow, non-stick frying pan. Spoon 2 tablespoons of mixture into the pan and swirl to cover the base. Cook for a few seconds, flip over and cook the second side. Repeat to make 8 pancakes in total.

125g (4 oz) plain flour

$1/2$ teaspoon salt

1 large egg, beaten

300 ml ($1/2$ pint) milk

125g (4 oz) frozen chopped spinach, thawed

vegetable oil, for frying

 REALLY EASY! 10 MINUTES MAKES 8 V

PANCAKES
STUFFING SUGGESTIONS

Try adding chopped herbs to the basic batter; cook and fill with one of the suggestions below. Roll up, sprinkle over a little grated cheese and heat through under the grill.

Chilli Con Carne (page 195)

Garlic Mushrooms (page 259)

Curried Beans (page 221)

Ratatouille (page 212)

Guacamole (page 240) **and sour Cream**

Mexican Topping (page 32)

Greek Yogurt with Crispy Onions (page 34)

Feta Cheese with Black Olive Dressing (page 33)

Potato and Mushroom Salad (page 60)
with a spoon of Hot Chilli Sauce (page 251)

White Bean Pâté (page 243)

Refried Beans (page 250) and sour cream

SWEET IDEAS

Sprinkle hot pancakes with a little caster sugar and top with one of the following:

Toasted marshmallows with melted chocolate

Mashed banana and Greek-style yogurt

Canned mandarin segments with condensed milk

Grilled peach slices with honey and flaked almonds

A squeeze of orange or lemon juice

BEAN AND CHEESE CASSEROLE

This bean stew is topped with breadcrumbs and finished in the oven. Try making this dish with any type of beans.

Preheat the oven to 190ºC, 375ºF, Gas 5. Heat one tablespoon of vegetable oil in a large saucepan and gently cook the onion, garlic and celery for 5 minutes until softened. Add the beans, tomatoes, herbs and 150 ml ($1/4$ pint) of water. Season to taste and simmer together for 10 minutes.

Transfer half the bean mixture into a casserole dish and place the cheese on top. Spoon over the remaining bean mixture.

Sprinkle over the breadcrumbs and bake for 15–20 minutes until golden.

2 tablespoons vegetable oil

1 onion, sliced

2 garlic cloves, chopped

1 celery stick, chopped

400g (14 oz) can mixed beans, drained

200g (7 oz) can chopped tomatoes

$1/2$ teaspoon dried mixed herbs

seasoning

125g (4 oz) cheese, grated

90g (3 oz) fresh breadcrumbs

EASY!

35 MINUTES

SERVES 2

V

CHEESY CRUST CASSEROLE

2 tablespoons olive oil

1 onion, roughly chopped

2 garlic cloves, finely chopped

1 small courgette (zucchini), thickly sliced

1 small aubergine (eggplant), cubed

1 yellow pepper (capsicum), diced

400g (14 oz) can chopped tomatoes and their juice

1 teaspoon dried thyme

seasoning

For The Cheese Crust

90g (3 oz) self-raising flour

1/2 teaspoon salt

30g (1 oz) vegetable suet

60g (2 oz) Cheddar cheese, finely grated

Aubergine (eggplant), courgette (zucchini) and pepper (capsicum) with tomatoes, topped with a delicious cheesy crust. The pastry top is very easy to make and if you don't have a rolling pin, try using a clean jar or bottle or pat out with your hands.

Preheat the oven to 200ºC, 400ºF, Gas 6. Heat the oil in a large frying pan and stir-fry the onion, garlic, courgette (zucchini), aubergine (eggplant) and pepper (capsicum) for about 8 minutes until softened and beginning to brown. Add the tomatoes and thyme and season to taste. Simmer gently for about 10 minutes.

Meanwhile **place** the ingredients for the crust into a large bowl. Add 5 tablespoons of cold water and bring to together to form a soft dough. Roll out on a lightly floured surface until large enough to cover your casserole dish.

Transfer the tomato mixture to a small casserole dish and lay the dough on top. Press the dough around the edges with your thumbs. Bake for 25 minutes until puffed and golden brown.

 EASY!

 45 MINUTES

 SERVES 2

 V

TOAD IN THE HOLE

Toad in the hole doesn't usually have onions in it, but I think they add flavour and texture to the dish. If you're a traditionalist, leave them out.

Preheat the oven to 200°C, 400°F, Gas 6. Sift the flour into a bowl with a little salt and pepper. Make a well in the centre and pour in the egg and half the milk. Beat to make a stiff batter and gradually work in the remaining milk. Set aside to rest for a few minutes while you fry the sausages.

Heat 1 tablespoon of oil in a large frying pan and cook the sausages and onion rings for 10 minutes until golden. Remove and drain. Place the remaining tablespoon of oil in a shallow, heatproof dish and place in the oven for a few minutes. Remove the dish from the oven and put in the sausages and onions. Pour over the batter and bake for 30 minutes until the batter has risen and is crisp and golden.

60g (2 oz) flour

seasoning

1 egg, beaten

150 ml (¼ pint) milk

2 tablespoons vegetable oil

1 onion, thinly sliced into rings

250g (8 oz) pork sausages

 EASY!

 50 MINUTES

 SERVES 2

VEGGIES IN THE HOLE

60g (2 oz) plain flour

seasoning

1 egg, beaten

150 ml (¹/₄ pint) milk

2 tablespoons
vegetable oil

1 large onion, sliced

125g (4 oz) baby carrots,
scrubbed and trimmed

60g (2oz) frozen peas

It is important to heat a little oil in the baking dish before you pour in the batter as it creates a seal and prevents sticking.

Preheat the oven to 200ºC, 400ºF, Gas 6. Sieve the flour into a bowl with a little salt and pepper. Make a well in the centre and pour in the egg and half the milk. Beat to make a stiff batter and gradually work in the remaining milk. Set aside to rest for a few minutes while you fry the vegetables.

Heat 1 tablespoon of oil in a large frying pan and cook the onion rings and carrots for 10 minutes until golden. Place the remaining tablespoon of oil in a shallow, heatproof dish and place in the oven. When hot remove the dish from the oven and put the carrot and onions into it.

Stir the peas into the batter and pour over the vegetables. Bake in the oven for 30 minutes until the batter has risen and is crisp and golden.

 REALLY EASY!
 50 MINUTES
 SERVES 2
 V

BEEF STEW AND DUMPLINGS

Although beef stew takes quite a long time, it is very easy and cheap to make, and you can leave the pot simmering away whilst you get on with some study. Use any root vegetables you fancy for this dish, try parsnips or turnips.

Season the flour and place in a small polythene bag, toss in the meat and shake the bag until the meat is evenly coated.

Heat the oil in a large saucepan and fry the beef and onion for 5 minutes until browned. Pour over the stock, cover and simmer for 1 hour.

Add the vegetables to the beef and simmer for 10 minutes whilst you make the dumplings. Place the flour, parsley, suet and a pinch of salt in a bowl. Add about 4 tablespoons of warm water and mix together to make a soft dough.

Shape into 6 small balls and drop into the stew. Cover and cook for 15–20 minutes until the meat, dumplings and vegetables are tender. Season to taste and serve.

2 tablespoons flour

seasoning

500g (1 lb) stewing steak, diced

1 tablespoon vegetable oil

1 large onion, sliced

900 ml (1$^{1}/_{2}$ pints) beef stock

1 large potato, diced

2 large carrots, thickly sliced

For The Dumplings

125g (4 oz) self-raising flour

1 teaspoon dried parsley

60g (2 oz) vegetable suet

REALLY EASY!

 90 MINUTES

 SERVES 2

VEGETABLE STEW WITH RED WINE AND DUMPLINGS

2 tablespoons olive oil

1 large onion, cut into large pieces

2 garlic cloves, quartered

1 large carrot, thickly sliced

2 parsnips, cut into bite-size pieces

1 leek, thickly sliced

1 tablespoon plain flour

450 ml ($^3/_4$ pint) vegetable stock

150 ml ($^1/_4$ pint) red wine

1 tablespoon tomato purée

seasoning

125g (4 oz) button mushrooms

For The Dumplings

90g (3 oz) self-raising flour

$^1/_2$ teaspoon salt

30g (1 oz) vegetable suet

1 tablespoon chopped fresh parsley

Fortunately vegetable suet is widely available in supermarkets so fluffy dumplings needn't be off the menu for vegetarians.

Heat the oil in a large saucepan and fry the onion, garlic, carrot, parsnip and leek together for 5 minutes until beginning to turn golden. Sprinkle on the flour and cook for 1 minute.

Gradually stir in the stock, wine, tomato purée and seasoning. Bring to the boil, cover and simmer for 10 minutes.

Meanwhile, **make** the dumplings. Sieve the flour and salt into a bowl. Stir in the suet, parsley and 5 tablespoons of water to form a soft dough. Shape into 8 small balls and add to the stew with the mushrooms.

Cover and simmer for 20 minutes until the vegetables are tender and the dumplings are cooked through. Season to taste and serve immediately.

EASY! **45** MINUTES SERVES **2**

HERBY SAUSAGES

90g (3 oz) fresh white breadcrumbs

60g (2 oz) Cheddar cheese, grated

1 tablespoon freshly grated Parmesan cheese

4 tablespoons chopped fresh chives

1 teaspoon English mustard

1 teaspoon dried sage

1 egg

seasoning

2 tablespoons plain flour

vegetable oil, for frying

These veggie sausages keep well in the fridge; simply cover and chill for a day or two before cooking.

Mix together the breadcrumbs, cheeses, chives, mustard, sage, egg and plenty of seasoning.

With floured hands, shape the mixture into 4 sausages.

Heat a little oil in a small frying pan and cook for 5–8 minutes until golden brown.

REALLY EASY!

10 MINUTES

SERVES 2

V

CHEESY BREAD AND BUTTER PUDDING

A delicious savoury version of bread and butter pudding.

Preheat the oven to 180°C, 350°F, Gas 4. Spread the butter on the bread and cut each slice into four triangles. Butter an ovenproof dish and arrange the bread in the dish sprinkling over the cheese, onion, parsley and a little seasoning between each layer.

Beat together the milk and egg and season lightly. Pour the liquid over the layers and bake in the oven for 30 minutes until well risen and golden.

EASY! 35 MINUTES SERVES 2 V

large knob of butter or margarine

6 slices white bread, crusts removed

180g (6 oz) Cheddar, or other cheese, grated

1 small onion, finely chopped

1 tablespoon chopped fresh parsley

seasoning

1 large egg

300 ml (¹/2 pint) milk

CREAMY VEGETABLE COBBLER

A mixture of broccoli, leek and peas in a cheese sauce, topped with a light scone mixture.

Preheat the oven to 220°C, 425°F, Gas 7. Heat the oil in a large saucepan and gently fry garlic, broccoli, leek and peas for 8 minutes until softened. Transfer the vegetables to a deep casserole dish.

Heat the butter in the same pan, stir in the flour and cook for 1 minute. Gradually add the milk, stirring until thickened. Bring to the boil and simmer gently for 3 minutes. Add all but a handful of the grated cheese, and stir until melted. Season to taste and pour over the vegetables.

Season the flour well with salt and pepper and then using just your fingertips, rub the butter into the flour until it resembles breadcrumbs. Stir in the parsley and milk and bring the mixture together to make a firm dough – add a little more milk if it feels too dry.

Shape the mixture into 8 balls and flatten each one gently with the palm of your hand. Arrange them on top of the casserole and sprinkle over the reserved cheese. Bake for 20 minutes until the cobbler topping is risen and golden.

1 tablespoon vegetable oil

1 garlic clove, finely chopped

250g (8 oz) broccoli, cut into florets

1 large leek, thickly sliced

250g (8 oz) frozen peas, thawed

30g (1 oz) butter or margarine

30g (1 oz) flour

300 ml (1/2 pint) milk

125g (4 oz) Cheddar cheese, grated

seasoning

For The Cobbler Topping

125g (4 oz) self-raising flour

60g (2 oz) butter or margarine, cut into small pieces

1 tablespoon chopped fresh parsley or 1 teaspoon dried

2 tablespoons milk

 REALLY EASY!

 55 MINUTES

 SERVES 2

FRENCH BREAD CASSEROLE

3 tablespoons olive oil

1 small onion, finely chopped

1 small aubergine (eggplant), diced

1 red pepper (capsicum), diced

1 yellow pepper (capsicum), diced

400g (14 oz) can plum tomatoes

60g (2 oz) black olives

few leaves fresh basil, roughly torn

seasoning

150g (5 oz) mozzarella cheese, sliced

1 small French stick, thickly sliced

This is a good way to use up French bread that is a little stale.

Preheat the oven to 220°C, 425°F, Gas 7. Heat 2 tablespoons of the oil in large pan and fry the onion, aubergine (eggplant) and peppers (capsicum) for 5 minutes until golden. Add the tomatoes and juice, olives and basil. Season to taste and simmer, covered, for 15 minutes until the vegetables are tender.

Transfer the mixture to an ovenproof dish and scatter over the mozzarella. Carefully arrange the bread slices on top, overlapping them to cover the casserole. Brush or drizzle the remaining oil over the bread and place in the oven for 10–15 minutes until golden brown and crisp.

 REALLY EASY!
 35 MINUTES
 SERVES 2
 V

TOMATO TART

It is very important that the mozzarella is well drained or the water will soak through the tart and make the pastry soggy.

Preheat the oven to 220°C, 425°F, Gas 7. Roll the pastry out into a large rectangle, about 5 mm (¹/₄ inch) thick. Using a small sharp knife, cut a border about 1 cm (¹/₂ inch) wide inside the rectangle – cut deep into the pastry, but not right through.

Spread the pesto sauce within the border and arrange the tomatoes on top. Season generously and scatter with the basil leaves. Drain the mozzarella well on kitchen paper and slice as thinly as possible.

Arrange the mozzarella slices on top of the tart and carefully transfer to a baking sheet/tray. Place in the oven for 15–20 minutes until the border has risen up to provide a puffy golden rim to the tart. Serve hot with a crisp green salad.

250g (8 oz) ready-made puff pastry, thawed if frozen

2 tablespoons ready-made pesto sauce

2 large tomatoes, thinly sliced

salt and freshly ground black pepper

handful of basil leaves

150g (5 oz) mozzarella cheese

 REALLY EASY!

 35 MINUTES

 SERVES 2

 V

CREAMY VEGETABLE TURNOVERS

1 large carrot, diced

60g (2 oz) frozen peas

125g (4 oz) small broccoli florets

knob of butter

1 tablespoon plain flour

300 ml (¹/₂ pint) milk, plus extra for brushing

1 tablespoon chopped fresh parsley

seasoning

250g (8 oz) ready-made puff pastry, thawed if frozen

You can make these pasties with any vegetables. Why not try making a cauliflower cheese version?

Preheat the oven to 220°C, 425°F, Gas 7. Place the carrot, peas and broccoli in a metal sieve and sit over a pan of boiling water. Cover with a lid or foil and steam gently for 5 minutes until tender but still crisp.

Meanwhile, **melt** the butter in a small pan. Stir in the flour and cook for 1 minute. Gradually beat in the milk to make a smooth sauce. Bring to the boil and simmer for 2 minutes until thickened. Stir the vegetables, parsley and seasoning into the sauce. Allow to cool.

Roll the pastry into 15cm (6 inch) squares and spoon in the vegetable mixture. Dampen the edges and fold over the pastry to form triangles, pressing down the edges to seal.

Transfer to a baking sheet/tray and brush with a little milk. Place in the oven for 15–20 minutes until puffed and golden brown. Serve with salad or vegetables.

EASY!

30 MINUTES

MAKES 4

V

FETA AND TOMATO PASTIES

Why not make double the recipe? These little pasties are great for a packed lunch.

Preheat the oven to 220°C, 425°F, Gas 7. Roll the pastry out into a large rectangle, measuring 30cm x 15cm (12 inch x 6 inch). Cut in half to give two 15cm (6 inch) squares.

Sprinkle the cheese on one half of each square and season well. Top with the chopped tomato and herbs. Beat together the egg and milk and brush a little around the edges. Fold over to make a triangle and press down well along the edges to seal.

Transfer to a baking sheet/tray and brush all over with the egg. Place in the oven for 15–20 minutes until puffed and golden. Serve with salad or vegetables.

250g (8 oz) ready-made puff pastry, thawed if frozen

180g (6 oz) feta cheese, crumbled

seasoning

1 large tomato, skinned, seeded and chopped

1 tablespoon chopped fresh parsley or chives

1 egg

2 tablespoons milk

 REALLY EASY!

 35 MINUTES

 SERVES 2

 V

BAKED BEAN AND CHEESE FLAN

400g (14 oz) can baked beans

20 cm (8 inch) shortcrust pastry case

150 ml (¼ pint) milk

1 egg

seasoning

60g (2 oz) Cheddar cheese, grated

This dish takes only minutes to prepare but is filling and tasty. Serve with a big helping of mashed potato.

Preheat the oven to 190°C, 375°F, Gas 5. Tip the can of beans into the pastry case.

Beat together the milk, egg and a little seasoning. Pour over the beans. Sprinkle the cheese on top and bake in the oven for 25–35 minutes, until set.

 REALLY EASY!

 35 MINUTES

 SERVES 2

 V

MUSHROOM PUFFS

Serve this tasty bread puff with a crisp green salad for a simple supper.

Preheat the oven to 190°C, 375°F, Gas 5. Beat together the eggs and milk with a little seasoning. Cut the crusts off the bread and tear the bread into small pieces. Add to the eggs and milk and leave to soak for a few minutes.

Heat the butter and gently cook the onion and garlic for 5 minutes until softened. Add the mushrooms and cook for a further 2–3 minutes. Season to taste.

Add the mushrooms to the bread mixture and stir well together. Transfer to a heatproof dish and cook in the oven for 20–30 minutes until puffed and golden brown.

2 eggs

7 tablespoons (100 ml) milk

seasoning

2 slices of bread

knob of butter or margarine

1 small onion, finely chopped

1 garlic clove, finely chopped

250g (8 oz) mushrooms, roughly chopped

REALLY EASY! 45 MINUTES SERVES 2 V

VEGETABLE SAMOSAS

1 large potato, diced

2 tablespoons vegetable oil

1 small onion, finely chopped

1 hot red chilli, seeded and finely chopped

1 teaspoon hot curry paste

125g (4 oz) frozen peas, thawed

juice of half a lemon

4 sheets filo pastry

These spicy samosas are brilliant for parties.

Preheat the oven to 220°C, 425°F, Gas 7. Cook the potato in boiling salted water for 10–12 minutes until just tender. Drain well.

Heat the oil in a large frying pan and cook the onion, chilli and curry paste for 2–3 minutes. Add the potatoes and peas and cook for a further 2–3 minutes, mashing down lightly with a fork. Remove from the heat. Stir in the lemon juice.

Work with 1 sheet of pastry at a time, keeping the rest covered with a damp cloth. Cut each sheet in half lengthwise to give 2 long strips. Put a spoonful of the mixture in one corner of each strip.

Fold the pastry and filling over at right angles to make a triangle and continue folding in this way along the strip of pastry to form a neat triangular parcel. Repeat with the remaining mixture.

Place on a baking sheet and brush with a little extra oil. Bake in the oven for 10–15 minutes until crisp and golden. Eat hot or cold.

 EASY!
 45 MINUTES
 MAKES 8
 V

QUICK COURGETTE AND LEEK PUFF TART

A crisp puff pastry case containing leeks, onion, courgettes (zucchini) and anchovies.

Preheat the oven to 220°C, 425°F, Gas 7. Melt the butter in a large frying pan and add the leek, onion and courgette (zucchini). Tear each anchovy in half and add to the pan with the oil from the can. Cook gently for about 10 minutes, until softened. Season well with black pepper.

Meanwhile, **roll** the pastry out into a large rectangle, about 1 cm ($^1/_2$ inch) thick. Using a small sharp knife, cut a border about $^1/_2$ cm ($^1/_4$ inch) wide inside the rectangle – cut deep into the pastry, but not right through.

Spread the courgette (zucchini) mixture onto the pastry, but within the border. Transfer to a baking sheet/tray and place in the oven for 15–20 minutes until the border has risen up to provide a puffy golden rim to the tart. Serve hot or at room temperature with a crisp green salad.

EASY!

35 MINUTES

SERVES 2

knob of butter or margarine

1 large leek, sliced

1 onion, sliced

2 courgettes (zucchini), sliced

can of anchovies in olive oil

freshly ground black pepper

250g (8 oz) ready made puff pastry, thawed if frozen

FILO PARCELS WITH FETA AND SPINACH

1 tablespoon olive oil

1 garlic clove, sliced

250g (8 oz) fresh spinach or 180g (6 oz) frozen leaf spinach, thawed

2 tomatoes, chopped

seasoning

4 large sheets filo pastry

30g (1 oz) butter, melted

125g (4 oz) feta cheese, crumbled

1 teaspoon cornflour

Filo pastry is very delicate and can crack easily if allowed to dry out. Dust lightly with flour and loosely cover with plastic wrap while it's waiting to be used.

Preheat the oven to 190°C, 375°F, Gas 5. Heat the olive oil in a large frying pan and cook the garlic, spinach and tomatoes together over a fairly high heat for 5 minutes. Season to taste, strain in a sieve, reserving the juices and leave for 10 minutes to cool.

Brush two sheets of pastry with some of the melted butter and place one on top of the other, buttered side uppermost. Cut in half lengthways to give two strips. Place a quarter of the spinach mixture in one corner of each pastry strip and crumble the feta cheese on top.

Fold the pastry and filling over at right angles to make a triangle and continue folding in this way along the strip of pastry to form a neat triangular parcel. Repeat with the remaining pastry and mixture to make four even-sized parcels.

Place on a baking sheet/tray and brush with the remaining melted butter and bake for 20 minutes until golden and crisp. Meanwhile, blend the cornflour with 1 tablespoon of water and stir into the reserved juices. Bring to the boil and simmer gently for 2 minutes. Serve the parcels with mashed potato and sauce.

 EASY!

 45 MINUTES

 SERVES 2

CHEESE AND HAM PASTIES

250g (8 oz) ready-made puff pastry, thawed if frozen

180g (6 oz) Cheddar or similar cheese, grated

1 tablespoon chopped fresh parsley or chives

1 egg

60g (2 oz) wafer thin ham

2 tablespoons milk

seasoning

Why not make double the recipe? These little pasties are good for a packed lunch.

Preheat the oven to 220°C, 425°F, Gas 7. Roll the pastry out into a large rectangle, measuring 30 cm x 15 cm (12 inch x 6 inch). Cut in half to give two 15 cm (6 inch) squares.

Sprinkle the cheese on one half of each square and season well. Top with the chopped herbs and the ham. Beat together the egg and milk and brush a little around the edges. Fold over to make a triangle and press down well along the edges to seal.

Transfer to a baking sheet/tray and brush all over with the egg wisk. Place in the oven for 15–20 minutes until puffed and golden. Serve with salad or vegetables.

REALLY EASY!

30 MINUTES

SERVES 2

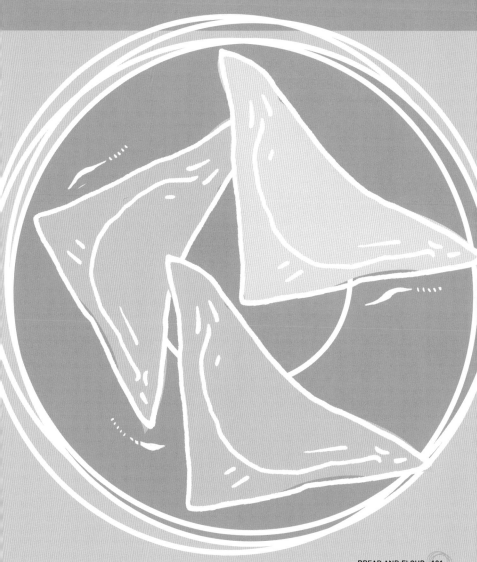

VEGETABLES
AND
BEANS

This food group is immense with shapes, colours, sizes and flavours stretching across the whole spectrum. You are sure to see different, odd-looking vegetables when you go to the shops, as the range of imported goods becomes wider and more varied each day. Once you've mastered home-grown produce, you might like to start experimenting with dishes that involve something more exotic, but for the moment stick to what you know.

INTRODUCTION

EAT SEASONALLY

It makes sense to base your meals around what is in season. Fresh fruit and vegetables in the peak of their season have far more flavour than those imported from hotter climates or grown in glasshouses to meet out of season demand. Not only do seasonal vegetables taste better, they're also a lot cheaper.

Here's a quick guide to when fruits and vegetables are at their seasonal best, and cheapest to buy.

Spring
broccoli, white cabbage, spring greens
----
cauliflower, mushrooms, leeks
----
new potatoes, asparagus, spinach, rhubarb, cucumber

Summer
courgettes (zucchini), peas, mangetout (snow peas), salad lettuces, broad beans, strawberries, watercress, radishes
----
peppers (capsicum), runner beans, globe artichokes, currants, peaches, nectarines
----
corn on the cob, celery, pak choi, aubergines (eggplants), blackberries, apricots

Autumn

marrows and squashes, plums

---

red cabbage, parsnips, swedes, potatoes,
turnips, pumpkins, apples, pears

---

leeks, shallots, Brussels' sprouts, oranges

Winter

beetroot, cabbages (red & white), Jerusalem
artichokes, nuts, figs

---

avocados, sweet potatoes

---

lemons, limes, pink grapefruit, marrows

SHOPPING

Buy fresh fruit and vegetables from your local market,
if you can, because the prices will be substantially lower
than in the supermarket or corner shop, and if you shop
on the way home from college, you're sure to pick up some
end-of-day bargains. As mentioned in the Eating Well
chapter, it is best not to store fresh vegetables for too long
so don't buy in bulk. If you only need two carrots, don't feel
you have to buy a whole kilogram.

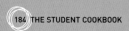

BEANS

It is very cheap and easy to buy dried beans and soak and cook them yourself, but it means you have to plan your meal at least a day in advance. There is such an excellent array of inexpensive canned beans on the shelves of supermarkets, that I'm not sure how many people actually take the time to cook dried beans. But for those of you who do want to, it is very important that you follow this guide carefully, as certain beans, particularly kidney beans, contain toxins that can make you quite ill if they are not destroyed by cooking:

TO COOK DRIED BEANS

Place the beans in a sieve or colander and rinse well, removing any pieces of grit. Tip into a large bowl, fill with cold water and leave for 8 hours, or overnight, to soak. Don't soak for over 24 hours or the beans will start to ferment.

Rinse well and place in a large saucepan. Cover with cold water, bring to the boil and boil rapidly for 15 minutes.

Drain and rinse well. Place in a saucepan and cover with clean cold water, bring to the boil and simmer, uncovered for 1–1½ hours until tender. Don't add salt as it can toughen the beans.

TOMATO AND BASIL SOUP

1 tablespoon olive oil

2 garlic cloves, finely chopped

1 small hot chilli, chopped

2 slices of white bread

400g (14 oz) can chopped tomatoes

pinch of sugar

seasoning

few leaves fresh basil, roughly torn

This delicious spicy soup can be served hot with crusty bread for a warming winter supper or chilled with cheese and crackers for a light supper in summer.

Heat the oil in a large saucepan, add the garlic and chilli and cook for 5 minutes until softened.

Meanwhile, **coarsely grate** the bread to make crumbs and add these to the pan with 300 ml ($^{1}/_{2}$ pint) of water and the can of chopped tomatoes. Stir in the sugar and seasoning, cover, and cook for 10 minutes until heated right through.

Stir in the basil leaves, divide into two bowls and serve with a good sprinkling of black pepper.

 REALLY EASY!
 15 MINUTES
 SERVES 2
 V

MUSHROOM SOUP WITH GARLIC CROUTONS

A creamy mushroom soup served with crunchy croutons which makes a filling supper dish.

Melt the margarine in a large saucepan and gently cook the garlic and spring onions for 3 minutes until softened. Add the flour and stir for 1 minute. Gradually beat in the stock. Bring to the boil, add the mushrooms, cover, and simmer for 30 minutes.

Meanwhile, make the croutons. **Heat** the oil in a small frying pan and cook the garlic for 5 minutes until golden, taking care not to burn it. Remove and discard the oil, toss in the bread and stir-fry for 2–3 minutes until golden. Drain on kitchen paper.

Stir the cream into the soup and season to taste. Heat through gently, pour into bowls and sprinkle with the croutons.

 EASY! 45 MINUTES SERVES 2 V

knob of margarine or butter

2 garlic cloves, finely chopped

4 spring onions, finely sliced

2 tablespoons plain flour

600 ml (1 pint) hot vegetable stock

250g (8 oz) mushrooms, finely chopped

150 ml ($^1/_4$ pint) single (pouring) cream

seasoning

For The Croutons

2 tablespoons olive oil

1 large garlic clove, quartered

1 thick slice of bread, cubed

CARROT AND ORANGE SOUP

600 ml (1 pint) vegetable stock

2 large carrots, grated

1 small onion, finely chopped

1 garlic clove, finely chopped

1 small potato, grated

juice of 2 oranges

1 tablespoon chopped fresh coriander or parsley

seasoning

This is an unbelievably easy, but tasty, soup that can happily be reheated the next day. It's fat free, so it's perfect for anyone counting their calories. Serve with hot buttered toast.

Place the stock, carrot, onion, garlic and potato together in a large saucepan. Bring to the boil, cover, and simmer for 20 minutes.

Stir in the orange juice and herbs and season to taste. Heat through and simmer for 5 minutes. Serve as it is, or if you prefer, liquidise, or pass through a metal sieve for a smoother, thicker soup.

 REALLY EASY!
 30 MINUTES
 SERVES 2
 V

ZESTY LENTIL SOUP

Lentils are a brilliant ingredient to keep close at hand. They don't need soaking, they're very nutritious and make the best soups and curries.

Heat the oil in a large saucepan and fry the celery, carrot, onion, garlic, ginger and cumin seeds for 5 minutes.

Add the lentils and stock, bring to the boil, cover and simmer for 30 minutes.

Stir in the lime juice and grated rind and season to taste. Serve with warm crusty bread.

1 tablespoon olive oil

1 celery stick, chopped

1 carrot, chopped

1 small onion, chopped

1 garlic clove, chopped

1 cm ($^1/_2$ inch) piece fresh ginger, grated

1 teaspoon cumin seeds

60g (2 oz) red lentils

900 ml (1$^1/_2$ pints) vegetable stock

grated rind and juice of a lime

seasoning

REALLY EASY!

35 MINUTES

SERVES 2

V

CREAMY RED PEPPER SOUP

2 red peppers
(capsicum), quartered
and seeded

2 tomatoes, halved

750 ml (1¼ pints)
vegetable stock

150g (5 oz) carton
Greek yogurt

1 tablespoon chopped
fresh coriander
or parsley

seasoning

This sweet, rich soup is so simple to make but tastes very sophisticated. Why not serve it to friends or for a special occasion? Try it with orange or yellow peppers for a change.

Arrange the peppers (capsicum) and tomatoes on a baking sheet and place under a preheated grill for 8 minutes, turning once, until softened. Carefully peel the skins from the peppers (capsicum) and tomatoes and discard.

Roughly chop the grilled vegetables and place in a saucepan with the stock. Cover and simmer for 20 minutes then push through a metal sieve.

Return to the pan and add the yogurt and coriander. Heat through without boiling, season to taste and serve with warm crusty bread.

 REALLY EASY!

 30 MINUTES

 SERVES 2

 V

MULLIGATAWNY

This spicy curry soup is sure to brighten up a rainy day.

Heat the oil in a large saucepan. Add the garlic, onion, potato and carrot and cook for 5 minutes until beginning to turn golden brown.

Stir in the curry paste, lentils and stock. Bring to the boil, cover and simmer for 20 minutes, stirring occasionally, until the vegetables and lentils are tender.

Mix the ground almonds with a little water to form a paste and add to the soup. Season to taste and serve immediately.

 REALLY EASY!

 25 MINUTES

 SERVES 2

2 tablespoons vegetable oil

1 garlic clove, finely chopped

1 onion, finely chopped

1 potato, cut into small dice

1 large carrot, cut into small dice

1 tablespoon curry paste

60g (2 oz) red lentils

600 ml (1 pint) vegetable stock

60g (2 oz) ground almonds

seasoning

CHEESE AND ONION SOUP

small knob of butter

1 large onion, chopped

1 tablespoon plain flour

600 ml (1 pint) milk

125g (4 oz) mature Cheddar cheese, grated

1 tablespoon wholegrain mustard

seasoning

A creamy rich soup made with onion, cheese and mustard.

Melt the butter in a large pan and cook the onion for 10 minutes until softened and golden. Stir in the flour and cook for 1 minute.

Gradually beat in the milk and bring to the boil. Stir in the cheese and mustard and heat until the cheese has just melted. Season to taste and serve with hot buttered toast or warm crusty bread.

 REALLY EASY!

 15 MINUTES

 SERVES 2

 V

SPINACH AND CHICK-PEA SOUP

Serve this hearty soup with thick slices of buttered toast for a filling meal.

Heat the oil in a large saucepan, add the onion and chilli and cook for 5 minutes until softened. Add the stock, spinach, tomatoes and chick-peas and bring to the boil. Cover and simmer for 15 minutes.

Season to taste and ladle into bowls. Serve with a swirl of olive oil and a good sprinkling of freshly ground black pepper.

2 tablespoons olive oil

1 large onion, sliced

1 small red chilli, seeded and diced

600 ml (1 pint) vegetable stock

250g (8 oz) frozen leaf spinach

2 tomatoes, skinned and diced

400g (14 oz) can chick-peas, drained

salt and freshly ground black pepper

PEPPERONATA

4 tablespoons olive oil

1 red pepper (capsicum), deseeded and sliced

1 yellow pepper (capsicum), deseeded and sliced

1 large onion, sliced

2 garlic cloves, sliced

2 tomatoes, skinned and quartered

1 tablespoon chopped fresh basil or parsley

salt and freshly ground black pepper

Serve this with crusty bread to mop up the juices or try with freshly cooked pasta or use to top a baked potato.

Heat the oil in a saucepan and add the peppers (capsicum), onion and garlic. Cover and simmer very gently, stirring occasionally, for 25 minutes until the vegetables are softened.

Add the tomatoes and cook for a further 15 minutes until tender. Stir in the parsley and season to taste. Serve hot or at room temperature.

 REALLY EASY!
 45 MINUTES
 SERVES 1
 V

CHILLI CON CARNE

A hot spicy mixture of beef, chillies, tomatoes and kidney beans.

Heat the oil in a large frying pan and cook the onion, garlic, chilli and mince for 5 minutes until the vegetables are softened and the meat is no longer pink.

Stir in the tomatoes, kidney beans, chilli powder and a little seasoning. Cover and simmer for 45 minutes.

Serve with ready-made tacos or boiled rice.

REALLY EASY! 50 MINUTES SERVES 2

1 tablespoon vegetable oil

1 onion, chopped

1 garlic clove, finely chopped

1 fresh chilli, finely chopped

250g (8 oz) lean minced beef

400g (14 oz) can chopped tomatoes

400g (14 oz) can red kidney beans, drained

2 teaspoons hot chilli powder

seasoning

MEXICAN CHILLI

1 tablespoon
vegetable oil

1 onion, finely chopped

1–2 red chillies, seeded
and finely chopped

1 garlic clove,
finely chopped

1 tablespoon paprika

1 teaspoon chilli powder

1 tablespoon tomato
purée

400g (14 oz) can red
kidney beans, drained

200g (7 oz) can chopped
tomatoes and their juice

1 teaspoon dried oregano

seasoning

Red kidney beans with onion, tomatoes, chilli and oregano – best served with rice.

Heat the oil in a large pan and cook the onion, chillies and garlic for 5 minutes until softened and lightly golden. Add the paprika and chilli powder and cook for 1 minute.

Stir in the tomato purée, beans, chopped tomatoes and oregano. Cover and simmer gently for 10 minutes. Season to taste and serve with rice.

 REALLY EASY! 20 MINUTES SERVES 2 V

CAULIFLOWER CHEESE

The secret of a good cauliflower cheese is to make sure that the cauliflower is not overcooked – it should be firm and even slightly crunchy rather than soft.

Place the florets in a colander and sit over a pan of boiling water. Cover with a lid or foil and steam for 5–7 minutes, until tender, but not mushy.

Meanwhile, **melt** the butter in a pan, stir in the flour and cook for 1 minute. Gradually beat in the milk to make a smooth sauce. If it does become lumpy, whisk it vigorously.

Bring the sauce gently to the boil and add about $^3/_4$ of the cheese and the mustard. Simmer for 1–2 minutes, until the cheese has melted and season to taste.

Transfer the cauliflower to a heatproof dish and pour over the cheese sauce. Scatter over the remaining cheese and place under a hot grill for 5 minutes until golden and bubbling.

1 cauliflower, cut into florets

30g (1 oz) butter or margarine

30g (1 oz) plain flour

300 ml ($^1/_2$ pint) milk

180g (6 oz) mature Cheddar cheese, grated

1 teaspoon English mustard

seasoning

EASY! 15 MINUTES SERVES 2

TOFU STIR-FRY

300g (10 oz) packet firm tofu

$^1/_2$ tablespoons vegetable oil

1 garlic clove, finely chopped

1 cm ($^1/_2$ inch) piece fresh root ginger, peeled and finely chopped

250g (8 oz) broccoli, cut into small florets

1 red pepper (capsicum), deseeded and cut into 2.5 cm (1 inch) pieces

1 tablespoon soy sauce

If the tofu is too wet it will crumble into the stir-fry rather than keep its shape, so it must be drained well. If you have a little more time, try deep frying the cubes of tofu before adding to the stir-fry, for a crispy, chewy texture.

Remove the tofu from the packet and place on 2 layers of kitchen paper. Put 2 more sheets on top and weigh down for 5 minutes with a saucepan or heavy chopping board. Cut into about twelve 2.5 cm (1 inch) cubes.

Heat the oil in a wok or large frying pan, add the garlic, ginger, broccoli and red pepper (capsicum) and stir-fry over a high heat for 4 minutes.

Add the tofu and cook for a further 3–4 minutes until the vegetables are tender but still crisp. Season with the soy sauce and serve immediately with noodles or rice.

EASY! SERVES 2

VEGETABLE SATAY

Satay sauce usually contains coconut and can be quite complicated to make. This an easy short-cut version which tastes great on almost any grilled vegetable.

Thread the vegetables onto skewers and brush lightly with oil. Season and place under a preheated grill for about 10 minutes, turning occasionally, until tender.

Mix together the peanut butter and Worcestershire sauce and stir in 3 tablespoons of the boiling water. Drizzle over the vegetable kebabs and serve on a bed of rice or with pitta bread and salad.

 REALLY EASY! 15 MINUTES SERVES 2

1 courgette (zucchini), thickly sliced

2 tomatoes, quartered

1 red pepper (capsicum), seeded and cut into 2.5 cm (1 inch) pieces

1 yellow pepper (capsicum), seeded and cut into 2.5 cm (1 inch) pieces

125g (4 oz) small broccoli florets

1 tablespoon vegetable oil

seasoning

For The Satay Sauce

4 tablespoons smooth peanut butter

1 tablespoon vegetarian Worcestershire sauce

CASSOULET

2 tablespoons
vegetable oil

1 onion, sliced

2 garlic cloves, chopped

1 celery stick, chopped

400g (14 oz) can mixed
beans, drained

200g (7 oz) can
chopped tomatoes

$1/2$ teaspoon dried
mixed herbs

seasoning

2 pork chops

60g (2 oz) fresh
breadcrumbs

A cassoulet is a French bean stew that's topped with breadcrumbs and finished in the oven. Try this recipe with any type of beans.

Preheat the oven to 190°C, 375°F, Gas 5. Heat one tablespoon of vegetable oil in a large saucepan and gently cook the onion, garlic and celery for 5 minutes until softened. Add the beans, tomatoes, herbs and 150 ml ($1/4$ pint) of water. Season to taste and simmer together for 10 minutes.

Meanwhile, fry the pork chops for 3–4 minutes on each side until lightly browned. Transfer half the bean mixture into a casserole dish and place the chops on top. Spoon over the remaining bean mixture.

Sprinkle over the breadcrumbs and bake for about 40 minutes until golden.

EASY!

1 HOUR

SERVES 1

SPINACH AND CANNELLINI BEAN STEW

This is one of those dishes that tastes even better the next day, it just needs a quick warm-through in a saucepan. If you can't get hold of fresh spinach, use frozen leaf spinach instead.

Heat the oil in a large saucepan and cook the bacon, onion and garlic for 2 minutes. Add the potato and stir-fry for a further 3 minutes.

Pour in the stock, bring to the boil and simmer, uncovered, for 30 minutes. Add the spinach and cannellini beans and cook for 10 minutes.

Season to taste and divide between two bowls. Swirl a little olive oil into each bowl and sprinkle over some freshly ground black pepper.

EASY! **55** MINUTES SERVES **2**

1 tablespoon olive oil, plus extra for serving

2 rashers streaky bacon, chopped (optional)

1 onion, chopped

1 garlic clove, finely chopped

1 very large potato, cut into chunks

1.2 litres (2 pints) vegetable or chicken stock

250g (8 oz) fresh leaf spinach

400g (14 oz) can cannellini beans, drained

salt and freshly ground black pepper

THAI CHICK-PEA CURRY

2 garlic cloves

handful of fresh coriander

1 small green chilli, seeded

1 tablespoon vegetable oil

2 potatoes, cut into small dice

400g (14 oz) can chick-peas, drained

2 tomatoes, cut into wedges

300 ml (1/2 pint) coconut milk

1 tablespoon soy sauce

pinch of sugar

seasoning

Chick-peas are often used as the base of Thai curries, and with the addition of typical flavourings, coriander and coconut, this recipe gives an aromatic, sophisticated-tasting curry that's actually very easy to make.

Use a heavy knife to chop together the garlic, chilli and coriander until blended into a paste.

Heat the oil in a large saucepan and fry the paste for a minute. Toss in the potato, chick-peas, tomatoes and coconut milk, cover with a lid and simmer for 15 minutes until the potatoes are tender.

Season to taste with the soy sauce, sugar, salt and pepper. Serve with rice or noodles.

 REALLY EASY!
 15 MINUTES
 SERVES 1
 V

PINEAPPLE AND BEANSPROUT STIR-FRY

Serve this stir-fry with boiled rice or egg noodles.

Heat the oil in a wok or large frying pan until very hot, and quickly fry the onion and ginger for 2 minutes. Toss in the pineapple chunks and juice, button mushrooms and five spice powder and stir-fry for 5 minutes.

Flavour with soy sauce and vinegar, toss in the beansprouts and cook for a further 3 minutes until the beansprouts have just wilted. Check the seasoning and serve immediately.

1 tablespoon vegetable oil

1 onion, thinly sliced

2.5 cm (1 inch) piece fresh ginger, grated

250g (8 oz) can pineapple chunks in natural juice

180g (6 oz) button mushrooms, halved

$1/2$ teaspoon five spice powder

1 tablespoon soy sauce

1 tablespoon vinegar

250g (8 oz) fresh beansprouts

seasoning

MIXED VEGETABLE GRATIN

2 tablespoons olive oil

2 courgettes (zucchini), thickly sliced

4 large flat mushrooms, thickly sliced

2 large tomatoes, thickly sliced

$1/2$ teaspoon dried oregano

60g (2 oz) Cheddar cheese, grated

seasoning

Large flat mushrooms give lots of flavour to this tasty dish of vegetables topped with grilled cheese.

Heat the oil in a large frying pan and cook the mushrooms and courgettes (zucchini) for about 5 minutes until softened. Add the tomatoes and oregano and cook for a further 5 minutes and season to taste.

Transfer the vegetables to a heatproof dish and sprinkle over the cheese and season. Place under a preheated grill for 5 minutes until bubbling and golden. Serve immediately with salad and bread.

REALLY EASY! SERVES 2

ORIENTAL PRAWN STIR-FRY

Fresh root ginger can be bought in most super-markets, just snap off a small piece and it won't cost much.

Heat the oil in a wok and quickly stir-fry the garlic and ginger for 2 minutes. Add the vegetables and prawns and cook for a further 5 minutes.

Add the soy sauce and 2 tablespoons of water and season to taste. Sprinkle in the sesame seeds and cook for 2 minutes until the vegetables are just tender and the stir-fry is piping hot. Serve with boiled rice or noodles.

 REALLY EASY!

 10 MINUTES

 SERVES 2

2 tablespoons vegetable oil

2 garlic cloves, chopped

1 cm (1/2 inch) piece fresh root ginger, peeled and finely chopped

125g (4 oz) button mushrooms, sliced

125g (4 oz) broccoli florets

60g (2 oz) frozen peas

125g (4 oz) large peeled prawns

2 tablespoons soy sauce

1 tablespoon sesame seeds

seasoning

BAKED BEAN AND LEEK HASH

2 tablespoons vegetable oil

500g (1 lb) potatoes, diced

---

1 large leek, finely chopped

400g (14 oz) can baked beans

60g (2 oz) Cheddar cheese, grated

---

seasoning

Baked beans are a stand-by in almost everyone's cupboard and they make a great addition to this hash.

Heat the oil in a large heavy-based frying pan. Add the potatoes, and cook, stirring, for 10 minutes, until semi-cooked.

Add the leeks, and continue to cook for 5 minutes, stirring, until the leeks have softened.

Stir in the beans, grated cheese and seasoning and cook the hash over a medium heat, until a crust forms on the bottom. Stir the hash to let the mixture brown throughout.

Turn the hash over, and pat down to form a cake. Cook until a crust forms on the bottom. Turn onto plates and serve.

REALLY EASY!   **20** MINUTES   SERVES **2**

STUFFED AUBERGINES

This dish cannot be prepared in advance, but once cooked can be covered and kept in the fridge for a couple of days and served cold with a crisp salad.

Preheat the oven to 200°C, 400°F, Gas 6. Cut the aubergine (eggplant) in half lengthwise and using a tablespoon, scoop out the flesh to leave a $^1/_2$ cm ($^1/_4$ inch) thick shell.

Finely chop the flesh with a heavy knife and place in a bowl with the breadcrumbs, egg, cheese, parsley and garlic. Season well and mix together.

Pile back into the shells, pressing down with the back of the spoon. Arrange the tomato layers on top and sprinkle with the dried oregano and little freshly ground black pepper.

Pour 4 tablespoons of water into a small roasting tin and carefully stand the aubergine (eggplant) halves in the water. Bake for 30–40 minutes until tender and golden brown on top.

1 large aubergine (eggplant)

2 slices of white bread, grated into crumbs

1 egg, beaten

60g (2 oz) mozzarella or Cheddar cheese, cut into small dice

2 tablespoons chopped fresh parsley

2 garlic cloves, finely sliced

2 large tomatoes, sliced

$^1/_2$ teaspoon dried oregano

freshly ground black pepper

 EASY!

 50 MINUTES

 SERVES 2

VEGETABLE KORMA

1 tablespoon
vegetable oil

- -

1 onion, finely chopped

- -

1 tablespoon curry paste

- -

500g (1 lb) mixed
vegetables cut into
bite-size chunks
e.g. carrot, potato,
broccoli, cauliflower,
peas

- -

400 ml (14 fl oz) can
coconut milk

- -

60g (2 oz) flaked
almonds

- -

seasoning

- -

This is great way of making use of leftover cooked vegetables – simply reduce the cooking time at step 2 to 5 minutes.

Heat the oil in a large saucepan and cook the onion over a fairly high heat for 5 minutes until golden brown. Stir in the curry paste and cook for 1 minute.

Add the vegetables and coconut milk, cover, and simmer for 15 minutes until the vegetables are tender. Meanwhile, place the almonds in a non-stick frying pan and dry-fry for 2–3 minutes, tossing the almonds until golden brown.

Season the curry to taste and sprinkle over the toasted almonds. Serve immediately with rice or naan bread.

 REALLY EASY!
 30 MINUTES
SERVES 2
 V

SPICY BEAN BURGERS

Burgers made with butterbeans and spinach and flavoured with garlic, chilli, cumin and coriander.

Heat the oil in a small saucepan and fry the onion, garlic and chilli for 5 minutes until softened.

Mash the beans well and place in a bowl with the spinach, breadcrumbs, cumin and coriander. Add the fried onion mixture and stir well together.

Season to taste and shape into four round burgers. Grill or shallow fry for a few minutes on each side until crisp and golden. Serve in burger buns with relish and salad.

 EASY! **20** MINUTES SERVES **2**

1 tablespoon vegetable oil

1 small onion, finely chopped

2 garlic cloves, finely chopped

1 small hot red chilli, finely chopped

400g (14 oz) can butterbeans

125g (4 oz) frozen chopped spinach, thawed

60g (2 oz) fresh breadcrumbs

1 teaspoon ground cumin

1 tablespoon chopped fresh coriander

seasoning

CHINESE-STYLE MIXED MUSHROOMS

1 tablespoon vegetable oil

1 hot red chilli, thinly sliced

2 garlic cloves, thinly sliced

1 bunch spring onions, thickly sliced on the diagonal

250g (8 oz) mixed mushrooms (shiitake, oyster, chanterelles etc.)

2 tablespoons soy sauce

4 tablespoons dry cider

150 ml (¼ pint) hot vegetable stock

1 teaspoon sesame oil

1 teaspoon cornflour

½ teaspoon five spice powder

A wonderfully quick and very tasty stir-fry of mushrooms. Serve with Chinese Egg Fried Rice (page 120).

Heat the vegetable oil in a wok or large frying pan. Add the chilli, garlic, spring onions and mushrooms and stir-fry over a high heat for 3 minutes.

Blend together the soy sauce, cider, stock, sesame oil, cornflour and five spice powder and pour over the mushrooms. Bring to the boil and simmer for 3 minutes until the mushrooms are just tender and the sauce has thickened. Serve immediately on a bed of egg-fried rice.

 REALLY EASY!

 10 MINUTES

 SERVES 2

 V

CAULIFLOWER TORTILLA

Spanish tortillas always contain potatoes, so although this does not technically qualify, it's every bit as tasty.

Plunge the cauliflower florets into boiling salted water for 3–4 minutes until just tender but still crisp. Drain.

Heat the oil in a small deep frying pan and cook the peas, chilli and garlic together for 5 minutes until soft. Add the cauliflower and stir-fry for 2–3 minutes.

Beat together the eggs, milk, parsley and seasoning. Pour over the vegetables, turn down the heat to the lowest setting and cook gently for about 8 minutes until the mixture is almost completely set – keep checking the underside to make sure it doesn't burn.

Use a spatula to carefully turn the tortilla over, or if it's a little tricky, place a plate over the pan, invert the tortilla onto the plate and then slide it back into the pan. Cook for a further 2 or 3 minutes until the underside is golden brown. Cut into wedges and serve.

250g (8 oz) cauliflower florets

2 tablespoons olive oil

125g (4 oz) frozen peas

1 small red chilli, seeded and finely chopped

1 garlic clove, finely chopped

4 eggs, beaten

2 tablespoons milk

1 tablespoon chopped fresh parsley or 1 teaspoon dried

seasoning

 REALLY EASY!

 30 MINUTES

 SERVES 2

RATATOUILLE

2 tablespoons olive oil

1 large onion, chopped

2 garlic cloves, finely chopped

250g (8 oz) ripe tomatoes, roughly chopped

1 small aubergine (eggplant), diced

2 courgettes (zucchini), thickly sliced

1 red pepper (capsicum), diced

2 tablespoons chopped fresh basil or 1 teaspoon dried

pinch of sugar

1 tablespoon tomato purée

seasoning

Any leftover ratatouille can be mixed with a little French dressing and served cold as salad.

Heat the oil in a large saucepan and cook the onion and garlic for 5 minutes until softened. Add the tomatoes and cook for a further 2 minutes.

Stir in the aubergine (eggplant), pepper (capsicum), courgette (zucchini), basil, sugar and purée. Cover and simmer gently for 30 minutes. Season to taste and serve.

 REALLY EASY!

 40 MINUTES

 SERVES 2

 V

CRISPY PARSNIP CAKES

Although the idea of boiled parsnips isn't everyone's cup of tea, these crispy patties really do taste brilliant.

Boil the parsnips in lightly salted boiling water for 10–15 minutes until tender. Drain well and mash with the butter, curry paste and seasoning. Leave to cool.

Shape into 4 round patties. Season the flour lightly and use to coat the patties. Dip them in the egg and then coat with the breadcrumbs.

Fry in hot oil for 3–4 minutes on each side until crisp and golden brown. Drain on kitchen paper and serve immediately with baked beans or crisp green salad.

4 large parsnips, peeled and diced

knob of butter

1 teaspoon mild curry paste

seasoning

2 tablespoons plain flour

1 egg, beaten

60g (2 oz) fresh breadcrumbs

vegetable oil, for frying

REALLY EASY! · 25 MINUTES · SERVES 2 · V

STUFFED MUSHROOMS

125g (4 oz) soft cheese
with garlic and herbs,
e.g. Boursin

2 tablespoons chopped
fresh parsley

1 tablespoon chopped
walnuts

2 tablespoons fresh
breadcrumbs

seasoning

2 large field mushrooms

Large flat mushrooms baked in the oven with a
topping of creamy garlic cheese, walnuts, parsley
and breadcrumbs.

Preheat the oven to 200°C, 400°F, Gas 6. Stir together
the soft cheese, parsley, walnuts and breadcrumbs
and season to taste.

Place the mushrooms on a baking sheet/tray and
pile the cheese mixture on top. Cook in the oven for
20 minutes until tender and golden. Serve immediately
with a crisp salad.

 REALLY EASY!
 25 MINUTES
 SERVES 1
 V

FALAFEL

Give refectory food a miss and pack some falafel in pitta pockets for your lunch. Or eat with Greek salad for a satisfying supper.

Mash the chick-peas, onion, chilli, cumin and coriander well together and season to taste. It may take a while to get the mixture soft enough to shape, as chick-peas can be quite dry and firm, but persevere and the mixture should come together.

Shape into 8 round balls and flatten into patties. Dip first into the beaten egg and then into the flour, shaking off any excess. Heat the oil in a frying pan and cook the patties for 2–3 minutes until golden brown. Drain well on kitchen paper.

400g (14 oz) can chick-peas, drained

half a small onion, very finely chopped

1 hot red chilli, very finely chopped

$1/4$ teaspoon ground cumin

1 tablespoon chopped fresh coriander

1 egg, lightly beaten

2 tablespoons flour

vegetable oil, for frying

seasoning

EGGS FLORENTINE

knob of butter

1 small onion, finely chopped

1 tablespoon plain flour

300 ml (½ pint) milk

125g (4 oz) frozen chopped spinach, thawed

1 tomato, skinned and roughly chopped

seasoning

2 eggs

Eggs baked in the oven on a bed of creamy spinach.

Preheat the oven to 200°C, 400°F, Gas 6. Heat the butter in a pan and gently cook the onion for 5 minutes until softened. Stir in the flour and cook for 1 minute.

Gradually beat in the milk to make a smooth sauce. Bring to the boil and simmer for 2–3 minutes until thickened. Stir in the spinach and tomato and season to taste.

Pour the mixture into a small heatproof dish and make 2 hollows. Crack an egg into each hollow and sprinkle over some freshly ground black pepper. Bake in the oven for 10–15 minutes until the eggs have set. Serve immediately with crusty bread.

 EASY!

 25 MINUTES

 SERVES 1

 V

BAKED COURGETTES

Halved courgettes (zucchini) filled with onion, chilli, sweetcorn, cream and Parmesan and baked in the oven.

Preheat the oven to 180°C, 350°F, Gas 4. Halve the courgettes (zucchini), scoop out the seeds with a teaspoon and discard. Arrange the courgettes (zucchini) side by side in a small ovenproof dish, cut side up.

Heat the oil in small pan and very gently cook the onion and chilli for about 5 minutes, until softened. Stir in the sweetcorn, egg, parsley, cream, Parmesan, and a little salt and plenty of black pepper.

Spoon the mixture over the courgettes (zucchini) and bake in the oven for 30 minutes until golden brown. Serve with salad and crusty bread.

4 courgettes (zucchini)

1 tablespoon vegetable oil

1 small onion, finely chopped

1 small chilli, seeded and finely chopped

180g (6 oz) sweetcorn

1 egg, beaten

1 tablespoon chopped fresh parsley

4 tablespoons double (thick) cream

2 tablespoons freshly grated Parmesan cheese

salt and freshly ground black pepper

SEEDY BEAN BURGERS

1 tablespoon vegetable oil

3 tablespoons pumpkin seeds

1 onion, finely chopped

1 small red chilli, seeded and finely chopped

400g (14 oz) can cannellini beans, drained and mashed

60g (2 oz) fresh breadcrumbs

1 egg, beaten

1 tablespoon lemon juice

2 tablespoons chopped fresh parsley

seasoning

vegetable oil, for frying

Fried pumpkin seeds have a delicious smoky flavour. For a tasty snack, dry-fry a handful in a non-stick pan for 2–3 minutes until golden and season with salt. Do watch out as they have a tendency to fly out of the pan as they get hot!

Heat the oil in a large frying pan and gently cook the pumpkin seeds, onion and chilli for 5 minutes. Remove from the heat. Stir in the beans, breadcrumbs, egg, lemon juice, parsley and seasoning.

Using floured hands, shape into four flat patties and shallow fry for 3–4 minutes on each side until crisp and golden brown. Remove with a slotted spoon and drain on kitchen paper. Serve in a bun with salad and mayonnaise or eat with ketchup and chips.

 REALLY EASY!
 15 MINUTES
 SERVES 2
 V

STUFFED PEPPERS

Red peppers (capsicum), stuffed with raisins, mushrooms, tomatoes, parsley and garlic, and baked in the oven.

Wash the rice well and cook in boiling water for 15–20 minutes until tender. Drain well and set aside to cool.

Preheat the oven to 200°C, 400°F, Gas 6. Twist the stalks out of the peppers (capsicum), turn them upside down and tap the bottom to shake out all the seeds.

Place the raisins, mushrooms, tomatoes, parsley, garlic, vinegar, honey and 2 tablespoons of olive oil in a large bowl. Add the rice, mix well together, and season to taste.

Spoon the mixture into the peppers (capsicum), pressing down with the back of the spoon. Carefully lay the peppers (capsicum) down in a small roasting tin, brush with the remaining oil, cover with foil and bake for 40 minutes until tender.

125g (4 oz) long grain rice

2 red peppers (capsicum)

2 tablespoons raisins

6 button mushrooms, sliced

2 tomatoes, diced

2 tablespoons chopped fresh parsley

2 garlic cloves, finely chopped

2 tablespoons white wine vinegar

1 tablespoon clear honey

3 tablespoons olive oil

seasoning

REALLY EASY!

70 MINUTES

SERVES 2

V

BAKED AUBERGINES

1 tablespoon
vegetable oil

seasoning

2 eggs, beaten

1 large aubergine
(eggplant), sliced into
1 cm (¹/₂ inch) rounds

1 quantity of Napolitana
sauce (page 85)

150g (5 oz) mozzarella
cheese, sliced

1 tablespoon freshly
grated Parmesan cheese

If you don't have time to make the tomato sauce your-self, use one of the many commercial brands available.

Preheat the oven to 180ºC, 350ºF, Gas 4. Heat the oil in a large frying pan. Season the eggs. Dip the aubergine (eggplant) slices in the beaten egg. Fry for 2–3 minutes on each side until golden brown. Remove with a slotted spoon and drain on kitchen paper.

Pour half the tomato sauce into a deep ovenproof dish and arrange a layer of aubergines (eggplant) on top. Scatter over the mozzarella and top with the remaining aubergine (eggplant) rounds. Pour over the rest of the tomato sauce and sprinkle with Parmesan. Bake in the oven for 30 minutes until golden and bubbling.

 REALLY EASY!
 40 MINUTES
 SERVES 2
 V

CURRIED BEANS

This is a wonderfully colourful and fragrant dish.
Serve with mashed or baked potatoes.

Heat the oil in a large saucepan and cook the onion,
garlic and ginger for 5 minutes until softened. Add the
curry paste and stir-fry for 2 minutes.

Stir in the beans, tomatoes, raisins and apple and
season well to taste. Gently simmer together for
20 minutes.

2 tablespoons
vegetable oil

1 onion, finely chopped

2 garlic cloves, finely
chopped

1 cm ($^1/_2$ inch) piece
fresh ginger, finely
grated

2 tablespoons hot curry
paste

400g (14 oz) can haricot
or cannellini beans,
drained

400g (14 oz) can chopped
tomatoes

60g (2 oz) raisins

1 apple, peeled and diced

seasoning

PAN FRIED COURGETTES WITH EGGS AND PARMESAN

2 tablespoons olive oil

1 courgette (zucchini), cut into sticks about 7.5 cm x 1 cm (3 x ½ inch)

1 large field or open cup mushroom, sliced

seasoning

1 tablespoon vinegar

2 eggs

1 tablespoon mayonnaise

30g (1 oz) Parmesan cheese, sliced thinly into flakes using a vegetable peeler

When poaching eggs, the vinegar is added to the water to help prevent the white spreading out too much. If you prefer you can top this dish with soft-boiled eggs in place of the poached.

Heat the oil in a large frying pan and when sizzling add the vegetables. Stir-fry over a high heat for 3–4 minutes until golden. Season well and transfer to a warm plate.

Half fill a small frying pan with water, add the vinegar and bring to the boil. Crack an egg into a cup and carefully slide it into the pan and repeat with the other egg. Poach for 3–4 minutes until the whites have set. Scoop out with a slotted spoon and drain on kitchen paper.

Spoon the mayonnaise onto the vegetables and top with the poached eggs. Scatter over the Parmesan and serve immediately.

 EASY!

 10 MINUTES

 SERVES **2**

 V

SALAD NIÇOISE

Salad Niçoise is an essential summertime recipe. It can be made a number of ways but generally contains hard-boiled eggs, anchovies and black olives. Serve with a French stick, some sparkling mineral water, and you'll have a fine feast.

Arrange the lettuce leaves on two plates and top with radishes, spring onion, eggs, tomato, anchovies and flakes of tuna. Scatter over the olives and a little seasoning and drizzle with olive oil and lemon juice.

REALLY EASY! 5 MINUTES SERVES 2

handful of small lettuce leaves such as lambs lettuce, watercress or baby spinach

1 bunch of radishes, halved

1 bunch of spring onions, roughly chopped

2 hard-boiled eggs, quartered

2 large firm tomatoes, quartered

10 anchovy fillets in oil, drained

200g (7 oz) can tuna in oil, drained and flaked

60g (2 oz) black olives

seasoning

2 tablespoons olive oil

juice of half a lemon

TUNA AND BEAN SALAD

400g (14 oz) can mixed beans, drained

half a cucumber, diced

2 tomatoes, diced

1 tablespoon chopped fresh parsley

1 red onion, thinly sliced into rings

180g (6 oz) can tuna in oil, drained

2 tablespoons olive oil

juice of half a lemon

1 garlic clove, crushed

seasoning

Layers of beans, cucumber, tomatoes, onions and tuna, moistened with a garlic lemon dressing.

Place the beans, cucumber, tomato and parsley in a bowl and mix well together. Transfer to a serving plate.

Arrange the onion rings and chunks of tuna on top of the beans. Whisk together the olive oil, lemon juice, garlic and plenty of seasoning. Drizzle over the salad and serve immediately.

REALLY EASY! 10 MINUTES SERVES 2

SNACKS
AND
STANDBYS

If you feel like a nibble, don't be tempted by crisps or chocolate. Dig deep into your cupboard and see if you can whip up a healthier, more filling snack to keep hunger at bay. However hard you might try, you'll sometimes fancy a bite to eat between meals. It may be because you missed a meal and need something to keep you going or perhaps it's just boredom. Whatever the reason here are a few easy ideas to help you combat a snack attack.

EGGY BREAD

The secret of eggy bread is to leave the bread soaking in the egg for as long as you can: 20 minutes is ideal. If you have any egg mixture left over, pour it on top of the bread as it is cooking in the pan.

Beat the egg and milk together in a shallow dish and dip in the bread. Press down with a spatula so the bread absorbs the liquid.

Heat a little oil in a frying pan and cook the bread for 3–4 minutes on each side until puffed and golden. Drain on kitchen paper and eat straightaway.

1 egg

2 tablespoons milk

2 slices of white bread

vegetable oil for frying

REALLY EASY!

30 MINUTES

SERVES 2

V

FRIED TOASTIES

knob of butter

2 slices of bread

60g (2 oz) grated cheese

1 tomato, sliced

For those of you who don't have access to a sandwich toaster, a decent non-stick frying pan is all you need to make crispy, golden sandwiches.

Butter the bread and make up a sandwich with the cheese and tomato with the butter on the outside.

Heat a non-stick frying pan. Carefully place the sandwich in the pan. Cook for about 3 minutes, pressing down gently with a spatula until golden brown underneath. Carefully, turn and cook other side. Eat immediately.

REALLY EASY!

5 MINUTES

SERVES 2

TOASTY FILLINGS

Any sort of cheese that melts makes a great toasty filling.
Try melting with any of the following:

Wholegrain mustard

Wafer thin ham

Red onion

Spring onions

Chives

Piccalilli

Warm baked beans or spaghetti hoops

Chopped garlic and a couple of torn basil leaves

Olive paste

Mayonnaise

Hot salsa (page 237)

OTHER FILLINGS TO TRY

Scrambled eggs and a little horseradish sauce

Roasted sweet potato and aubergine salad (page 61)

Diced avocado

Tomato and mayonnaise

Spanish tortilla (page 58)

Macaroni cheese (page 74)

Fried bacon and maple syrup

BARBECUED SPARE RIBS

2 tablespoons flour

seasoning

500g (1 lb) pork spare ribs

For The Barbecue Sauce

1 tablespoon dark soy sauce

1 tablespoon tomato purée

2 tablespoons clear honey

2 garlic cloves, finely chopped

1 cm (½ inch) piece fresh ginger, peeled and grated

juice of an orange

1 teaspoon English mustard

Some supermarkets sell spare ribs cut into small 'mini' ribs. If you can buy them, they are excellent for snack meals.

Place the flour, a little seasoning and the ribs together in a plastic bag. Shake the bag to coat the ribs.

Mix together all the sauce ingredients. Shake any excess flour off the ribs, dip into the sauce and place on a foil lined grill pan.

Place under a hot grill for about 30 minutes, turning and basting frequently with the remaining sauce until brown, shiny and cooked through. In the summer these ribs can be cooked on a barbecue.

 REALLY EASY!

 35 MINUTES

 SERVES 2

HAMBURGERS

Home-made hamburgers are so quick and cheap to make that it's really not worth buying them ready-made, and they freeze well too.

Place all the ingredients in a bowl and mix well together. Shape the mixture into 4 large, round patties.

Pop under a medium grill for around 8 minutes on each side until cooked through. Serve in sesame seed buns with salad and mustard.

500g (1 lb) lean minced beef

1 teaspoon Worcestershire sauce

1 small onion, finely chopped

1 tablespoon chopped fresh parsley

seasoning

TOMATO AND BREAD

1 ripe tomato

thick slice of bread,
e.g. ciabatta or rustic-
style country bread
or use the crust from
a sliced white loaf

2 fresh basil leaves
(optional)

extra virgin olive oil

coarse salt

This is a classic peasant snack from southern Italy. The field workers and farmers take a chunk of bread, handful of tomatoes and flask of olive oil out with them and assemble it for their lunch. My mother often gave me this as a snack after school and it's still a favourite standby of mine.

Cut the tomato in half and place the halves cut side down on the bread. Squash the tomatoes into the bread so that the juices and seeds soak in and the flesh breaks up a little. Roughly tear the basil leaves, if using, and scatter them on top. Drizzle over about a tablespoon of olive oil and sprinkle with salt.

 REALLY EASY!
 5 MINUTES
 SERVES 1
 V

MUSHROOM FRITTATA

A frittata is a spongy Italian omelette which, like the Spanish tortilla, is cooked slowly, cut into wedges and eaten hot or cold. Leftover frittata can be cut into chunks, simmered for a few minutes in a simple tomato sauce and served with buttered new potatoes and salad.

Mix together the eggs, breadcrumbs, garlic, parsley, and Parmesan and season well.

Heat the olive oil in a frying pan and cook the mushrooms for 4–5 minutes until softened. Tip in the egg mixture and smooth over with a spatula.

Cook slowly for about 5 minutes, until golden underneath. Carefully turn over and cook the other side until golden.

4 eggs, beaten

2 slices white bread, grated

1 garlic clove, sliced

2 tablespoons chopped fresh parsley

1 tablespoon freshly grated Parmesan cheese

2 tablespoons olive oil

125g (4 oz) mushrooms, sliced

seasoning

REALLY EASY!

 15 MINUTES

 SERVES 2

 V

BUFFALO CHICKEN WINGS

1 small onion, very finely chopped

2 garlic cloves, crushed

1 tablespoon clear honey

2 tablespoons vegetable oil

3 tablespoons tomato ketchup

2 tablespoons Worcestershire sauce

few drops of Tabasco sauce

12 chicken wings

Chicken wings baked with a spicy, devilled sauce. You won't be able to eat these without licking your fingers.

Preheat the oven to 200°C, 400°F, Gas 6. Place the onion, garlic, honey, vegetable oil, tomato ketchup, Worcestershire sauce and Tabasco together in a small saucepan. Simmer together for 5 minutes.

Place the chicken wings on a baking sheet/tray and brush all over with the sauce. Bake for about 30 minutes, basting occasionally with sauce, until cooked through and golden brown.

REALLY EASY!

40 MINUTES

SERVES 2

WELSH RAREBIT

This method may not be true to the original which is rather time consuming, but it tastes almost as good. Top each slice with a poached egg to make Buck Rarebit.

Beat together the cheese, mustard, Worcestershire sauce and butter to make a paste.

Spread on the toast and place under the grill for 3 minutes until bubbling and golden.

60g (2 oz) Cheddar cheese, grated

1 teaspoon English mustard

1 tablespoon Worcestershire sauce

small knob of butter

2 slices of toast

 REALLY EASY! 5 MINUTES SERVES 1 V

SCRAMBLED EGGS ON TOAST

2 eggs

2 tablespoons milk

salt and freshly ground black pepper

knob of butter

2 thick slices hot buttered toast

$^1/_2$ tablespoon freshly grated Parmesan cheese

A brilliant snack at any time of the day. Try adding different flavourings or ingredients such as chopped fresh herbs, a spoonful of tartare sauce, chopped ham, or diced tomatoes. Of course if you're celebrating the end of term, the classic addition to scrambled eggs is smoked salmon.

Lightly beat together the eggs, milk and seasoning.

Melt the butter in a small pan. Toss in the eggs and stir with a chopstick or fork until just set, but still a little runny, taking care not to over cook.

Turn onto the hot toast and sprinkle with a little grated Parmesan and a sprinkling of black pepper.

 REALLY EASY!

 5 MINUTES

 SERVES 1

 V

COURGETTE WHEELS WITH HOT SALSA

As a child, whenever I complained of feeling peckish, my mother used to whip up these golden wheels in about 5 minutes.

Mix together the tomatoes, chilli, garlic, onion, coriander, olive oil and seasoning and set aside whilst you fry the courgettes (zucchini).

Beat together the egg, milk and a little seasoning. Heat 1 cm ($^1/_2$ inch) of oil in a large frying pan. Season the flour. Dip the courgettes (zucchini) first into the flour, shake of any excess, dip into the egg and then fry for 2 minutes on each side until golden. Drain on kitchen towel and serve immediately with the hot salsa.

REALLY EASY! 15 MINUTES SERVES 2

1 egg

2 tablespoons milk

seasoning

vegetable oil, for frying

2 tablespoons flour

1 large courgette (zucchini), thinly sliced

For The Salsa

250g (8 oz) ripe tomatoes, finely chopped

2 small chillies, finely chopped

2 garlic cloves, finely chopped

1 small onion, finely chopped

1 tablespoon chopped fresh coriander

1 tablespoon olive oil

seasoning

CORN ON THE COB

1 corn cob

knob of butter

salt

Make the most of the juicy cobs of corn that are cheap and available in the summer months. You can flavour the butter with herbs, garlic or chilli, if you wish, but I prefer to serve it plain.

Peel back the husks, remove the silky threads and trim the stem. Bring a large pan of water to the boil, but do not add salt as it hardens the kernels during cooking.

Cook in the boiling water for 15 minutes, until the corn is bright yellow. Remove with a slotted spoon, smother with butter and sprinkle with salt. Eat immediately, using your fingers.

 REALLY EASY!
 15 MINUTES
 SERVES 1
 V

SWEETCORN FRITTERS

These crisp little fritters are quickly made from store cupboard ingredients.

Beat together the eggs, milk, self-raising flour and salt until smooth. Stir in the sweetcorn.

Heat 1 cm ($^1/_2$ inch) vegetable oil in a large frying pan and carefully drop in large spoonfuls of the mixture. Cook for 3–4 minutes on each side until crisp and golden. Serve with mayonnaise or make a quick topping by stirring some chopped chives into Greek yogurt.

2 eggs

4 tablespoons milk

90g (3 oz) self-raising flour

$^1/_2$ teaspoon salt

275g (10 oz) can sweetcorn, drained

vegetable oil, for frying

 REALLY EASY! **20** MINUTES SERVES **2** V

GUACAMOLE

1 ripe avocado

juice of half a lemon

1 small garlic clove, finely chopped

1 tablespoon olive oil

a few drops of Tabasco sauce

1 ripe tomato, skinned and diced (optional)

seasoning

A lovely smooth avocado dip that goes well with snack crackers, crisps, toasted French bread or vegetable sticks.

Mash all the ingredients together well and season to taste.

 REALLY EASY!

 5 MINUTES

 SERVES 1

 V

HUMMUS

Tahini is sesame seed paste and can be bought in health food shops and selected supermarkets if you prefer. You can use smooth peanut butter in its place. Hummus will keep covered in the fridge for a few days and is delicious spread thickly on hot buttered toast.

Mash together the chick-peas and garlic until fairly smooth. Gradually beat in the olive oil to give a creamy consistency.

Stir in the tahini, lemon juice and seasoning, adding more, or less, than the given amounts, to suit your taste.

400g (14 oz) can chick-peas, drained

2 garlic cloves, crushed

6 tablespoons olive oil

4 tablespoons tahini

juice of a lemon

seasoning

REALLY EASY!   5 MINUTES   SERVES 2

TSATZIKI

5 cm (2 inch) piece cucumber, coarsely grated

1 garlic clove, finely chopped

1 tablespoon finely chopped onion

150 ml ($^1/_4$ pint) Greek-style yogurt

1 tablespoon chopped fresh mint

seasoning

A fresh tasting dip of cucumber, garlic, mint and yogurt. Serve with warm pitta bread.

Mix all the ingredients together well and season to taste. Serve immediately.

 REALLY EASY!

 5 MINUTES

 SERVES 1

 V

WHITE BEAN PÂTÉ

This pâté is delicious served on garlic toast. Simply toast slices of French bread on both sides, rub the top surface with a cut clove of garlic and drizzle over a little olive oil. Keep any pâté that is left over covered, in the fridge for 1–2 days.

Heat the olive oil in a saucepan, add the garlic and rosemary and cook very gently for 5 minutes until the garlic is lightly golden.

Drain the beans, reserving the liquid. Add the beans to the pan with 2–3 tablespoons of the liquid and mash down well with a fork to make a rough purée. Add more liquid if needed and continue to cook for about 5 minutes until soft and creamy. Season to taste and eat warm or cold.

3 tablespoons olive oil

3 garlic cloves, finely chopped

1 teaspoon chopped fresh rosemary (optional)

400g (14 oz) can cannellini or butter beans

salt and freshly ground black pepper

REALLY EASY! 15 MINUTES SERVES 4

PIPERADE

1 tablespoon olive oil

1 red onion, sliced

1 garlic clove, finely chopped

1 large red pepper (capsicum), deseeded and sliced

4 eggs

4 tablespoons milk

2 tablespoons chopped fresh parsley

seasoning

This is a classic French dish which is a cross between an omelette and scrambled eggs, with a savoury filling.

Heat the oil in a large frying pan and gently cook the onion, garlic and pepper (capsicum) for about 8 minutes until softened.

Beat together the eggs, milk, parsley and seasoning and add to the pan.

Scramble together for 2 minutes until the eggs are just cooked. Serve with salad, a baked potato or on hot buttered toast for a quick snack or light lunch.

REALLY EASY!

15 MINUTES

SERVES 1

V

FRIED MUSHROOMS

These mushrooms make a delicious snack if served on a thick slice of buttered toast. Top with a fried egg for an even tastier and more substantial snack.

Heat the butter in a small frying pan and gently cook the onion and mushrooms for 5 minutes until golden. Stir in the Parmesan and season to taste. Tip the mixture onto the hot toast and eat.

small knob of butter

half an onion, finely chopped

125g (4 oz) mushrooms, sliced

1 tablespoon freshly grated Parmesan cheese

seasoning

thick slice of hot buttered toast, to serve

SESAME PRAWN TOASTS

125g (4 oz) prawns

2.5 cm (1 inch) piece
fresh root ginger, grated

1 garlic clove,
finely chopped

2 teaspoons cornflour

seasoning

1 egg white

4 slices white bread,
crusts removed

2 tablespoons sesame
seeds

vegetable oil, for frying

If you've ever tried these delicious tit-bits as a starter in a Chinese restaurant, like me you probably wondered how they were made. They are actually really simple to make yourself, and taste just as good as the ones that cost a fortune.

Finely chop the prawns with a heavy knife and mix together in a bowl with the ginger, garlic and cornflour. Season well.

In a separate bowl, **whisk** the egg white with a fork until frothy. Tip in the prawn mixture and blend well together.

Spread evenly onto the bread and cut each slice into 4 fingers or triangles. Sprinkle over the sesame seeds, and press firmly in place.

Heat 1 cm (^{1}/2 inch) of oil in a large frying pan and cook the fingers, prawn-side down first, for 2–3 minutes on each side until crisp and golden. Serve immediately.

 EASY!
 10 MINUTES
 SERVES 2

SCOTCH PANCAKES

Turn these brilliant Scotch pancakes into American ones by skipping the sultanas and lemon and adding a handful of fresh blueberries or raspberries and drizzling them with maple syrup before serving.

Sieve the flour, baking powder, sugar and salt into a bowl. Add the eggs and half the milk and beat with a wooden spoon until smooth.

Beat in the remaining milk and the melted butter to give a thick batter. Stir in the sultanas and lemon rind, if using, and leave to rest for about 5 minutes.

Heat a little oil in a large frying pan and drop in large spoonfuls of batter. Cook for a couple of minutes until bubbles rise to the surface and the pancakes are golden underneath. Flip over and cook the other side. Drain on kitchen paper and serve in a stack.

250g (8 oz) self-raising flour

1 teaspoon baking powder

30g (1 oz) sugar

pinch of salt

2 eggs, beaten

300 ml ($\frac{1}{2}$ pint) milk

45g ($1\frac{1}{2}$ oz) butter or margarine, melted

30g (1 oz) sultanas

grated rind of half a lemon (optional)

oil, for frying

REALLY EASY! 20 MINUTES SERVES 3 V

POTATO SKINS

2 potatoes, unpeeled

oil, for frying

salt

Save the flesh scooped out of the potatoes to make another dish such as potato pancakes (page 253), corned beef hash (page 49) or fish cakes (page 48). Americans traditionally serve skins with sour cream but there are lots of ways to eat them - grate over a little cheese, sprinkle with spring onions and pop under the grill to melt the cheese. Or try serving them with a delicious dip such as guacamole or tsatziki (pages 240 and 242).

Halve the potatoes lengthwise and boil in lightly salted water for 15 minutes. Drain well and pat dry. Use a spoon to scoop out the potato flesh, leaving a shell about 1 cm (^{1}/$_2$ inch) thick. Cut each shell into 3 or 4 strips.

Heat about 5 cm (2 inches) of vegetable oil in a heavy saucepan and fry the skins for 2–3 minutes until crisp and golden. Sprinkle with a little salt and serve.

REALLY EASY!

20 MINUTES

SERVES **2**

NACHOS

Try serving this Mexican snack with guacamole and sour cream for a light supper.

Empty the tortillas into a heatproof dish and pour over the chopped tomatoes. Sprinkle over the chilli and seasoning and place under a medium grill for 5–7 minutes until heated through.

Scatter the cheese over the top and return to the grill. Raise the heat and cook for a further 2–3 minutes until the cheese is bubbling. Eat immediately.

REALLY EASY! **15** MINUTES SERVES **1** V

125g (4 oz) pack tortilla chips

200g (7 oz) can chopped tomatoes, drained

1 mild green chilli, seeded and finely chopped

seasoning

60g (2 oz) Cheddar, grated

REFRIED BEANS

knob of butter or
1 tablespoon of
vegetable oil

1 onion, chopped

2 garlic cloves,
finely chopped

200g (7 oz) can chopped
tomatoes, drained

400g (14 oz) can kidney
beans, drained

1/2 teaspoon chilli powder

salt

Use these tasty beans as a filling for baked potatoes, pancakes or pack into a ready-made taco shell (which are readily available in supermarkets), with some crisp lettuce and a dollop of sour cream.

Heat the butter in a frying pan and gently cook the onion and garlic for 5 minutes until softened. Add the chopped tomatoes and heat through.

Add the beans a handful at a time, mashing them down roughly with a fork.

Season with chilli powder and salt and heat through.

 REALLY EASY! 10 MINUTES SERVES 2 V

HOT CHILLI SAUCE

This sauce is an essential standby. Stir it into pasta sauces, scrambled eggs, and serve on the side of countless plainer dishes for added flavour. If you have a liquidiser or a hand-held blender this sauce is incredibly quick to make, but the hand-chopped version, though a little rougher, is still very easy.

Push a fork into a tomato and hold in the flame of a gas ring for few seconds, turning until the skin blisters. Peel off the skin and discard. Repeat with the remaining tomatoes. If you do not have a gas cooker, place the tomatoes under a hot grill instead. Cut the tomatoes into quarters, scoop out and discard the seeds.

If you have a blender, **whizz** together the tomatoes, garlic, onion, chillies and parsley until smooth. If not, place them on a board and chop together with a heavy knife for as long as you can stand, until well-blended and fairly smooth.

Heat the vegetable oil in a frying pan, add the mixture and cook for about 10 minutes, stirring until thick and pulpy. Season well to taste and serve hot or cold.

4 tomatoes

1 garlic clove, roughly chopped

1 onion roughly, chopped

2 hot red chillies, seeded and roughly chopped

2 tablespoons chopped fresh parsley

1 tablespoon vegetable oil

seasoning

REALLY EASY! — 25 MINUTES — MAKES 1 CUP — V

HASH BROWNS

1–2 cold boiled potatoes

vegetable oil, for frying

salt

What do you eat if all you have in the house is a potato – and worse still, a cooked one? Simple, make a batch of crispy hash browns and serve with a dollop of brown sauce.

Coarsely **grate** the potato into a bowl and sprinkle with salt. At this stage you may choose to add other flavourings such as onion or parsley.

Shape the mixture firmly into flat ovals. Heat 1 cm (1/2 inch) of oil in a small frying pan and cook the hash browns for 3–4 minutes on each side until crisp and golden.

Drain on kitchen paper and eat immediately. They can be reheated under a hot grill.

REALLY EASY!

10 MINUTES

SERVES 1

V

POTATO PANCAKES

These fluffy pancakes can be eaten hot with baked beans or a fried egg for a light lunch or cold as a snack. Try adding different ingredients such as chopped ham, parsley, spring onions, or use Parmesan in place of Cheddar.

Cook the potatoes in boiling, salted water for 10–15 minutes, until tender.

Mash well with the butter, milk and cheese. Stir in the flour and season to taste. Use your hands to shape into about 8 round pancakes about 1 cm (¹/₂ inch) thick.

Place under a preheated grill and cook gently for about 5 minutes on each side until golden brown. Take care when turning the pancakes over as although they develop a crust on the outside, they are still soft inside.

500g (1 lb) potatoes, cubed

knob of butter

2 tablespoons milk

60g (2 oz) Cheddar cheese, grated

60g (2 oz) plain flour

seasoning

 EASY! 25 MINUTES SERVES 2 V

FRIED MOZZARELLA

150g (5 oz) mozzarella cheese

2 tablespoons plain flour

1 egg, beaten

seasoning

4 tablespoons fresh breadcrumbs

1 tablespoon chopped fresh parsley

vegetable oil, for frying

This snack is extra special if you use the mini balls of mozzarella that you can buy in supermarkets. Make sure the oil temperature is correct, if it is too hot, the breadcrumbs will brown too quickly before the cheese has melted in the centre. Likewise, if the oil is not hot enough, the cheese will melt and fall apart before the coating has become crisp and golden.

Drain the mozzarella well on kitchen paper. Cut into bite-size pieces and toss in the flour.

Beat the egg with a little seasoning and mix the breadcrumbs with the parsley.

Dip the floured pieces into the beaten eggs and then the breadcrumbs. Make sure they are completely covered in crumbs.

Heat 4 cm (2 inch) of oil in a deep pan until a cube of bread turns golden in 1 minute. Fry the cheese bites for 1 minute until crisp and golden. Drain on kitchen paper and eat immediately.

 EASY!

 10 MINUTES

 SERVES 1

 V

AUBERGINE APPETISER

Serve this appetising pâté with warm pitta bread and some strong black olives for a flavour-packed snack or starter. For a quick way to skin and seed tomatoes, see Hot Chilli Sauce recipe (page 251).

Grill the aubergine (eggplant) for about 20 minutes, turning occasionally until the skin is soft and blackened.

Meanwhile, **heat** 1 tablespoon of the oil in a small frying pan and cook the onion and garlic for 5 minutes until softened.

Peel the skin from the aubergine (eggplant) and discard. Mash the flesh with a fork and stir in the onion mixture, remaining olive oil, tomatoes, lemon juice, coriander and plenty of seasoning.

1 large aubergine (eggplant), halved

2 tablespoons olive oil

1 small onion, very finely chopped

2 garlic cloves, very finely chopped

2 ripe tomatoes, skinned, seeded and very finely chopped

juice of half a lemon

2 tablespoons chopped fresh coriander or parsley

salt and freshly ground black pepper

 EASY!
 35 MINUTES
 SERVES 2
 V

COURGETTE FRITTERS

1 large courgette (zucchini), grated

1 small onion, finely grated

1 small egg

4 tablespoons plain flour

$^1/_2$ teaspoon salt

vegetable oil, for frying

These little fritters are so delicious you may want to make double the quantity!

Place the courgette (zucchini) and onion in a large bowl. Stir in the egg followed by the flour and salt.

Heat a little oil in a frying pan and drop in a heaped tablespoon of the mixture, spread out thinly with the back of the spoon and cook for 2–3 minutes on each side until crisp and golden. Drain on kitchen paper and serve with Hot Chilli Sauce (page 251).

REALLY EASY! 10 MINUTES SERVES 2

SPINACH FRITTERS

This is a Spanish tapas dish that you can eat just as a snack or as an accompaniment to grilled meat or fish or with rice as part of a vegetarian meal.

Beat together the egg, chilli, nutmeg, Parmesan and seasoning. Mix with the spinach and breadcrumbs and shape into 4 round patties.

Heat a little oil in a frying pan and cook the fritters for 3–4 minutes on each side until crisp and golden.

REALLY EASY! · 10 MINUTES · SERVES 2 · V

1 egg

1/2 teaspoon chilli powder

pinch nutmeg

2 tablespoons freshly grated Parmesan cheese

seasoning

350g (12 oz) spinach, cooked if fresh or thawed if frozen, squeezed dry

45g (1 1/2 oz) fresh breadcrumbs

olive oil, for frying

MELTED RED ONION TOASTS

2 tablespoons olive oil

2 red onions,
thinly sliced

1 garlic clove,
thinly sliced

seasoning

1 thick slice
country bread

1 tablespoon mayonnaise

60g (2 oz) mozzarella or
Cheddar cheese,
thinly sliced

Try and buy red onions for this recipe as they are milder than ordinary onions and have a sweet flavour.

Heat the oil in frying pan, add the onions and garlic cook very gently for 15 minutes until very soft and golden brown. Season well.

Toast the bread and spread with the mayonnaise. Pile on the onions, cover with the cheese and place under a preheated grill for 2–3 minutes until the cheese is bubbling. Eat immediately.

 REALLY EASY!
 25 MINUTES
 SERVES 1
 V

GARLIC MUSHROOMS

Serve with warm French bread for a delicious snack or starter.

Heat the butter until foaming, but not brown. Toss in the mushrooms and garlic and cook for 2 minutes.

Add the lemon juice and seasoning, cover with a lid and cook gently for 5 minutes.

Remove the lid and cook for a further 5 minutes, until softened. Stir in the parsley and serve.

30g (1 oz) butter

125g (4 oz) small button mushrooms

1 large garlic clove, finely chopped

1 teaspoon lemon juice

seasoning

1 teaspoon chopped fresh parsley

 15 MINUTES

 SERVES 1

REALLY EASY!

APPLE AND CHEESE MUFFINS

small knob of butter

1 dessert apple, sliced

1 tablespoon salted peanuts, roughly chopped

1 muffin, split open

30g (1 oz) blue cheese, e.g. Stilton, blue brie, dolcellate

Pan-fried apples and nuts with blue cheese makes a great combination for any bread base. Try with crumpets or toast.

Melt the butter in a small frying pan and when sizzling toss in the apple and nuts. Cook over a fairly high heat for 4–5 minutes until golden.

Spoon onto the open muffin halves and crumble over the cheese. Pop under a preheated grill for 2–3 minutes until bubbling. Eat at once!

 REALLY EASY!
 15 MINUTES
 SERVES 1
 V

CHEESE PUFFS

This snack is perfect for a midnight feast.

Preheat the oven to 190°C, 375°F, Gas 5. Mix together the cheese, egg, mustard and a little seasoning.

Butter the bread then spread thickly with the cheese mixture. Cut each slice into 4 triangles and place on a baking sheet/tray. Cook in the oven for about 10 minutes until puffed and golden brown.

180g (6 oz) finely grated cheese

1 egg, beaten

1 teaspoon English mustard

seasoning

knob of butter or margarine

4 slices bread

BANANA SANDWICH

2 slices bread

1 ripe banana

1 tablespoon clear honey

Toast the bread on both sides. Break the banana into 2 or 3 pieces and lay on top of the toast. Roughly mash into the toast with a fork then drizzle over the honey. Replace top slice of toast, cut in half and eat while still warm.

REALLY EASY!

5 MINUTES

SERVES 1

INDEX